D0880922

Springer Compass International

Series Editors
Steven S. Muchnick
Peter Schnupp

David R. Musser
Alexander A. Stepanov

The Ada®Generic Library
Linear List
Processing Packages

Springer-Verlag
New York Berlin Heidelberg
London Paris Tokyo Hong Kong

David R. Musser
Computer Science Department
Rensselaer Polytechnic Institute
Troy, NY 12180

Alexander A. Stepanov
Software Technology Laboratory
Hewlett-Packard Laboratories
Palo Alto, CA 94303

Cover: Pastel on paper (1984), John Pearson

Library of Congress Cataloging-in-Publication Data
Musser, David R.
    The Ada generic library : linear list processing packages / David
R. Musser, Alexander A. Stepanov.
        p.   cm.
    Includes bibliographical references.
    ISBN 0-387-97133-5
    1. Ada (Computer program language)   2. List processing (Electronic
computers)   I. Stepanov, Alexander A.   II. Title.
QA76.73.A35M87   1989
005.13′3—dc20   89-21683

ADA® is a registered trademark of the U.S. Government ADA Joint Program Office.

Printed on acid-free paper.

Camera-ready text provided by the authors using the LaTeX Macros system of document preparation.
Printed and bound by R.R. Donnelley & Sons, Harrisonburg, Virginia.
Printed in the United States of America.

9 8 7 6 5 4 3 2 1

ISBN 0-387-97133-5 Springer-Verlag New York Berlin Heidelberg
ISBN 3-540-97133-5 Springer-Verlag Berlin Heidelberg New York

Preface

The purpose of the Ada Generic Library is to provide Ada programmers with an extensive, well-documented library of generic packages whose use can substantially increase productivity and reliability. The construction of the library follows a new approach, whose principles include the following:

- Extensive use of generic algorithms, such as generic *sort* and *merge* algorithms that can be specialized to work with many different data representations and comparison functions.

- Building up functionality in layers (practicing software reuse within the library itself).

- Obtaining high efficiency in spite of the layering (using Ada's *inline* compiler directive).

This volume contains eight Ada packages, with over 170 subprograms, for various linear data structures based on linked lists.

The Ada Generic Library project was begun in 1987 at General Electric Research and Development Center, with support also from GE Aerospace and GE Aircraft Engines. We thank Susan Mickel and William Novak of GE Western Systems for useful suggestions and comments on early versions of the library; and Joel Sturman, Dave Oliver, and Art Chen of GE Research and Development Center for their support of this project and for permission to publish this description in book form. Some of the material in this volume is adapted from our papers "A Library of Generic Algorithms in Ada," *Proc. of 1987 ACM SIGAda International Conference*, Boston, December, 1987, and "Generic Programming," to appear in *Proc. 1988 International Symposium on Symbolic and Algebraic Computation, Lecture Notes in Computer Science*, Springer-Verlag, July, 1988. Preparation of the final manuscript has been supported by Rensselaer Polytechnic Institute.

We have prepared this volume to serve two different purposes. The first and more obvious is as a resource for professional Ada programmers, whom we hope will find the packages useful in building application programs or in some cases further construction of generic libraries. For this audience there is the question of obtaining and making use of the library with one's local Ada system; further information on this point is given below. Secondly, those interested in programming methodology, software reusability, and more general software engineering concerns may find a number of interesting aspects in our approach to library construction, as detailed in Chapter 1. Here we would like to point out that our approach is not limited to the Ada language; we believe Ada has both advantages and disadvantages when compared to other languages as a base for generic software library construction. We have also experimented extensively with two other languages, Scheme and C++; somewhat different techniques are required in each language, but we have been able to maintain the same basic approach.

Some words of caution about current Ada compilers

To the programmer who would like to make use of this library, a warning must be given concerning the current state of Ada compilers. When we began developing these packages, we immediately discovered that a number of Ada compilers had difficulty in handling the heavily layered generics we use in structuring the library. Initially (in early 1987) we were able to compile the packages with only one compiler: the Digital Equipment Corporation Ada compiler for VAX/VMS systems. Two compilers for SUN workstations and three IBM PC based compilers that we tried all would abort during compilation, usually with some cryptic diagnostic about internal errors. (One of the most popular—and most expensive—PC based compilers went into an infinite loop!) By the end of 1987, possibly in response to our trouble reports, Telesoft Corporation produced a new version of its Ada compiler with improved handling of generics, capable of compiling the entire library as it appears in this volume.

With the DEC and Telesoft Ada compilers, extensive testing has been carried out (many of the test cases are detailed in this volume), and we believe programmers using those systems can be confident of being able to make productive use of the library. But we must warn that it may not even be possible to compile the library with other compilers. At this writing we have not had time to work directly with other compiler vendors, but the possibility of including the library in the Ada Validation Suite is under discussion, so that improvements would have to be made in handling of generics in order to have future compilers validated. That may not happen for some time, however, and we hope that in the meantime that all Ada compiler vendors will give some attention to these packages.

Obtaining the source code on diskette

The complete source code for these packages is contained within this volume, but it can also be obtained on 5 1/4 inch diskettes in IBM PC format. Information on ordering the source code appears at the end of this volume. Since there may not presently be any IBM PC based Ada compiler capable of compiling the full library, it is intended that the diskettes and an IBM PC compatible computer be used to transfer the files to another environment using some standard file transfer program such as Kermit.

Contents

II   Restricted-Access Data Structures

Part I

Unrestricted-Access Data Structures

1

Introduction

Most work on improving software productivity and reliability has focused on language issues or on program development tools or environments. While these are important issues, the real key to software productivity, and to the reliability and maintainability of the product, may well be the construction and widespread use of libraries of highly reusable software components. The importance of reusable software components is rapidly gaining recognition, and libraries of considerable magnitude have been developed in the Ada language. Unfortunately, in most libraries little advantage has been taken of the facilities of Ada for *generic* programming. Thus, as in previous libraries developed in older languages such as Fortran or Jovial, there is little flexibility and much unnecessary duplication of code and documentation, causing difficulties in learning to use the library and in maintaining and extending it.

The goal of the Ada Generic Library project is to provide Ada programmers with an extensive, well-structured and well-documented library of generic packages whose use can substantially increase productivity and reliability. We have developed a new technical approach to organizing such a library, which we call the *generic programming approach*, and have produced the first phase of the library following these principles. We believe these principles, which are quite different from those on which other libraries have been founded, have broad applicability to the goal of reusable and highly reliable software components.

As a simple example of the generic programming approach, consider the task of choosing and implementing a sorting algorithm for linked list data structures. The merge sort algorithm can be used and, if properly implemented, provides one of the most efficient sorting algorithms for linked lists. Ordinarily one might program this algorithm directly in terms of whatever pointer and record field access operations are provided in the programming language. Instead, however, one can abstract away a concrete representation and express the algorithm in terms of a small number of basic operations. In this case, we need just the operations **Next** and **Set_- Next** for accessing the next cell in a list, **Is_End** for detecting the end of a list, **Copy_Cell** for copying information from one cell into another, and **Test** for comparing the information in two cells according to some ordering relation.

For a particular representation of linked lists, one then obtains the corresponding version of a merge sorting algorithm by instantiating the basic operations to be subprograms that access that representation. Different representations yield different concrete algorithms, but the source code for the generic algorithm is the same in each case; the differences at the concrete level, and the optimizations required in each case (e.g., for dead code removal) are taken care of by the Ada compiler and linker. The Test operation need not be instantiated at this stage; by leaving it and the type of data elements as generic parameters, one obtains a partially instantiated algorithm that can still be used in many different ways depending on the element type and ordering.

In the initial phase of the Ada Generic Library project, we have applied the generic programming approach on a small but nontrivial scale, to produce a collection of *linear data structure* manipulation facilities, specifically for a number of linked-list representations. The data structures and algorithms included have been selected based on their well-established usefulness in a wide variety of applications. This volume contains and documents eight Ada packages (about 170 subprograms) which serve as building blocks that can be plugged together to produce extensive collections of operations on several linear data structures. The resulting components perform very common and useful operations such as building, maintaining, sorting and searching lists of information. The selection of operations for the largest package, Singly_Linked_Lists, is largely based on the facilities available in Common Lisp [9].

We hope to expand the library and provide additional volumes of documentation. Some obvious candidates for inclusion would be packages for other linked-list and vector representations of linear data structures, rectangular data structures, trees, and graphs. Aside from such expansion, there are a number of other directions in which this work might be carried further. These are discussed briefly in the concluding section of this chapter.

1.1 Principles behind the library

The key points of the generic programming approach can be summarized as follows:

- Use generic algorithms and data types to express general capabilities

  - *A generic algorithm is a template for generating an algorithm by plugging in a set of types and basic operations*

- Generate components for specific applications by instantiation

  - *Small amount of source code yields large number of useful instances*

  - *Library users can easily generate new components*

- Ensure component quality to much higher level than by usual means

  - *Get it right at generic level*

  - *To show correctness of an instance just need to show actual parameters meet their requirements*

- Provide highly detailed and cross-referenced documentation

  - *New kinds of classifications for generic components (based on abstraction mechanisms used)*

The most important technical idea of our approach is that of generic algorithms, which are a means of providing functionality in a way that abstracts away from details of representation and basic operations. Instead of referring directly to the host language facilities, generic algorithms are defined in terms a few primitive operations that are considered to be *parameters*. By plugging in actual operations for these parameters, one obtains specific instances of the algorithms for a specific data structure. By carefully choosing the parameterization and the algorithms, one obtains in a small amount of code the capability to produce many different useful operations. It becomes much easier *and much more reliable* to obtain the operations needed for a particular application by plugging components together than it is to program them directly.

1.2 Relation to software engineering goals

The notion of generic programming is not entirely new, but to our knowledge there has not been any previous attempt to construct a general software library founded on this idea. Most work on development of data structure facilities has focused on data abstraction (a.k.a. abstract data types, information hiding, data encapsulation) [2, 10]. Older program libraries, written in Fortran or other languages without the facilities for generic programming, could not take advantage of the algorithm abstractions that were known. But even the recent improvements in abstraction facilities in contemporary programming languages, such as Ada, have not precipitated widespread use of algorithmic abstraction. G. Booch [1] makes some use of generic algorithms for list and tree structures, but almost as an afterthought in a chapter on utilities. Some of our goals are similar to those of the "parameterized programming" approach advocated by J. Goguen [3], but a fundamental difference is that Goguen mainly addresses meta-issues—namely, how to manipulate theories—while our primary interest is in building useful theories to manipulate.

Although the present volume represents only a small step, we believe that extensive use of our approach could eventually be a major factor in achieving some of the important goals of software engineering, e.g.,

Data Abstractions	System_Allocated_Singly_Linked
Data types with operations	User_Allocated_Singly_Linked
defined on them	{Instances of rep. abstractions}
Algorithmic Abstractions	Sequence_Algorithms*
Families of data abstractions	Linked_List_Algorithms
with common algorithms	Vector_Algorithms
Structural Abstractions	Singly_Linked_Lists
Intersections of	Doubly_Linked_Lists*
algorithmic abstractions	Vectors*
Representational Abstractions	Double_Ended_Lists
Mappings from one structural	Stacks
abstraction to another	Output_Restricted_Deques

TABLE 1.1. Classification of Abstractions and Example Ada Packages

- *Programmer productivity* can be enhanced, compared to the usual practice of hand-crafting software components for each new application.

- *Reliability* of software produced as instances of generic algorithms can be substantially higher (very few bugs have been encountered during development of the library itself).

- *Efficiency* equal to that of hand-coded components can be obtained by careful structuring of code and the use of compiler optimization directives.

For the benefits of the generic programming approach to software reusability to be fully realized, great care must be exercised in selecting and structuring algorithms, especially in determining how they are parameterized and how they are used to develop more concrete levels of the library. In the following sections, some of the main issues in structuring the library are discussed in more detail.

1.3 Structure of the library

The key structuring mechanism used in building the library is *abstraction*. We discuss four classes of abstractions that we have found useful in structuring the library, as shown in Table 1.1, which lists a few examples of packages in the library. Each of these Ada packages has been written to provide generic algorithms and generic data structures that fall into the corresponding abstraction class. (The packages marked with a * are not included in this release of the library.) These classes are defined as follows:

1.3.1   DATA ABSTRACTIONS

Data abstractions are data types and sets of operations defined on them (the usual definition); they are abstractions mainly in that they can be understood (and formally specified by such techniques as algebraic axioms) independently of their actual implementation. In Ada, data abstractions can be written as packages which define a new type and procedures and functions on that type. Another degree of abstractness is achieved by using a generic package in which the type of elements being stored is a generic formal parameter. In our library, we program only a few such data abstractions directly—those necessary to create some fundamental data representations and define how they are implemented in terms of Ada types such as arrays, records and access types. Three such packages, which we refer to as "low-level data abstraction packages," are presented in Chapters 3, 4, and 5. Most other data abstractions are obtained by combining existing data abstraction packages with packages from the structural or representational classes defined below.

1.3.2   ALGORITHMIC ABSTRACTIONS

These are families of data abstractions that have a set of efficient algorithms in common; we refer to the algorithms themselves as *generic algorithms*. For example, in our library there is a package of generic algorithms for linked-lists; in a future release there will be a more general package of sequence algorithms whose members can be used on either linked-list or vector representations of sequences. The linked-list generic algorithms package contains 31 different algorithms such as, for example, generic merge and sort algorithms that are instantiated in various ways to produce merge and sort subprograms in structural abstraction packages such as singly-linked lists and doubly-linked lists.

Thus in Ada one programs generic algorithms in a generic package whose parameters are a small number of types and access operations—e. g.,

```
generic
   type Cell is private;
   with function Next(S : Cell) return Cell;
   with procedure Set_Next(S1, S2 : Cell);
   with function Is_End(S : Cell) return Boolean;
   with function Copy_Cell(S1, S2 : Cell) return Cell;
package Linked_List_Algorithms is
   . . .
```

The subprograms in the package are algorithms such as **Merge** and **Sort** that are efficient when **Next**, **Set_Next**, etc., are instantiated with constant time operations.

1.3.3 STRUCTURAL ABSTRACTIONS

Structural abstractions (with respect to a given set of algorithmic abstractions) are also families of data abstractions: a data abstraction A belongs to a structural abstraction S if and only if S is an intersection of some of the algorithmic abstractions to which A belongs. An example is singly-linked lists, the intersection of sequence, linked list, and singly-linked list algorithmic abstractions. It is a family of all data abstractions that implement a singly-linked representation of sequences; it is the connection with more detailed structure of representations that inspires the name "structural abstraction." (In this volume, the Singly_Linked_Lists package (Chapter 6) is actually programmed just in terms of the Linked_List_Algorithms package.)

Note that, as an intersection of algorithmic abstractions, such a family of data abstractions is smaller than the algorithm abstraction classes in which it is contained, but a *larger* number of algorithms are possible, because the structure on which they operate is more completely defined.

Programming of structural abstractions can be accomplished in Ada with the same kind of generic package structure as for generic algorithms. The Singly_Linked_Lists package contains 66 subprograms, most of which are obtained by instantiating or calling in various ways some member of the Linked_List_Algorithms package. In Ada, to actually place one data abstraction in the singly-linked-lists family, one instantiates the Singly_Linked_Lists package, using as actual parameters a type and the set of operations on this type from a data abstraction package such as System_Allocated_Singly_Linked that defines an appropriate representation.

1.3.4 REPRESENTATIONAL ABSTRACTIONS

These are mappings from one structural abstraction to another, creating a new type and implementing a set of operations on that type by means of the operations of the domain structural abstraction. For example, stacks can easily be obtained as a structural abstraction from singly-linked-lists, and this is carried out in Ada using generic packages in a manner that will be demonstrated in Part 2. Note that what one obtains is really a family of stack data abstractions, whereas the usual programming techniques give only a single data abstraction.

1.4   Selection from the library

The first observation we would make is that proper classification of software components for maximum usability may well depend more on *internal structure* than on functional (input-output) behavior. In searching the library, the programmer needs to know not only whether there is a subprogram that performs the right operation, but also what kind of data representation it uses (if it is not a completely generic algorithm), since in all but the simplest cases it will be used in a particular context that may strongly favor one representation over another.

Experienced programmers will sometimes want to use generic algorithms directly, instantiating the generic access operations to be subprograms accessing a particular data representation. Although generic, these algorithms are tailored to be used with data representations with particular complexity characteristics, such as linked-list- versus array-like representations, and the programmer must be aware of these issues.

This is not to say that intelligent use of the library necessarily requires the programmer to examine the bodies of the subprograms. If construction of the library is, as we have recommended, algorithmically-driven and draws upon the best books and articles on algorithms and data structures, then it should be possible to develop sufficiently precise and complete *selection criteria* based on the advice in those books and articles. Again, the preparation of these selection criteria and other documentation must be done very carefully and thoroughly to make later usage by programmers as simple as possible. (The selection criteria contained in this volume are mainly for choosing between different subprograms within a package; they should be supplemented with criteria for choosing between different packages.)

1.5   Using the library

The packages in the Ada Generic Library are intended to be included in a local site's Ada library structure (using the library mechanism supported by the Ada system in use locally), so that a programmer can use them simply by including appropriate with statements in his or her source code. In most cases the programmer will not use packages from the four abstraction classes directly; instead it is simpler to use what we call Partially Instantiated Packages, or PIPs. Each PIP effectively "plugs together" a low-level data abstraction package with a structural or representational package, presenting a generic package interface in which the only generic parameters are the element type and perhaps some size or other control parameters. In this release of the library there are twelve PIPs provided, one for each combination of one of the three low-level data abstraction packages in Chapters 3, 4, and 5 with the Singly_Linked_Lists package in Chapter 6 or one of the three packages in Part 2. PIPs are discussed further in Chapter 7.

1.6   Future directions

Aside from the obvious possibilities for expansion of the library to include other data structures and algorithm classes, there are two main areas in which we would like to carry this work forward. One is to explore the relation between generic programming and the *design stage* of a more conventional software development approach. By programming at an abstract level and carefully organizing libraries of software components, one can accomplish some of the tasks one ordinarily thinks of as software design, but the result is more than just a design. With the help of a language capable of expressing generic algorithms, a compiler that can automatically construct and optimize diverse instances of generics, and library maintenance tools, all of which are provided by good Ada systems, we effectively have *executable designs*, in a stronger sense than any previous approaches of which we are aware. We believe this aspect of generic programming deserves much further study.

The other area in which we are see strong potential for generic programming is mathematical specification and verification of software components. In [7], we explore some of the key issues that arise in this area. Although the documentation of the initial library in this volume is informal, and we have not yet carried out formal specification and verification of the library components, we believe that this task would be both mathematically interesting and practically useful.

On the mathematical side, the correctness of generic algorithms offers greater challenges and less tedium than concrete algorithms, for often one must create the appropriate abstract concepts in terms of which one can effectively express and reason about the behavior of an algorithm or collection of algorithms. The nature of the problem of verifying generic algorithms should be attractive to researchers in computer science and mathematics, whereas the problem for concrete algorithms is often regarded as so tedious as to be worth doing only if most of the work can be done with an automated reasoning system.

On the practical side, the considerable work of composing a formal specification and carrying out a detailed proof of correctness at a generic level is compensated by the ease with which one is then able to deal with the correctness of many distinct instantiations. While it is often difficult to justify the amount of effort required for formal verification of concrete programs, except in the case of software used in life-critical systems, the possibility of verifying components in generic software libraries may open the way for the benefits of this technology to become widely available.

1.7   References

[1] G. Booch, *Software Components in Ada.* Benjamin/Cummings, 1987.

[2] O.-J. Dahl, E. W. Dijkstra, and C. A. R. Hoare, *Structured Programming*, Academic Press, 1972.

[3] J. Goguen, "Parameterized Programming," *Transactions on Software Engineering*, SE-10(5):528-543, September 1984.

[4] A. Kershenbaum, D. R. Musser and A. A. Stepanov, "Higher Order Imperative Programming," Computer Science Dept. Rep. No. 88-10, Rensselaer Polytechnic Institute, Troy, New York, April 1988.

[5] Donald E. Knuth, *The Art of Computer Programming*, Vols. 1-3, Addison-Wesley, 1968, 1969, 1973.

[6] D. R. Musser and A. A. Stepanov, "A Library of Generic Algorithms in Ada," *Proc. of 1987 ACM SIGAda International Conference*, Boston, December, 1987.

[7] D.R. Musser and A.A. Stepanov, "Generic Programming," invited paper, to appear in *Proc. 1988 International Symposium on Symbolic and Algebraic Computation, Lecture Notes in Computer Science*, Springer-Verlag, July, 1988.

[8] R. Sedgewick, *Algorithms*, Addison-Wesley, 1983.

[9] G. L. Steele, *Common LISP: The Language*, Digital Press, 1984.

[10] N. Wirth, *Algorithms + Data Structures = Programs*, Prentice-Hall, 1976.

2

Linear Data Structures

2.1   Sequences

The first phase of the Ada Generic Library, Linear Data Structures, can be described in terms of the different data structures that are implemented or planned, most of which are relatively simple and familiar structures such as linked lists, vectors (one dimensional arrays), stacks, queues, deques, etc. However, a highly unifying way to organize one's understanding of these structures and the algorithms associated with them is in terms of the mathematical notion of (finite) *sequences*. A future version may include a **Sequences** package of generic algorithms, but for now we discuss sequences just as a way of understanding many aspects of linked-list and vector representations.

For a given data type T, the set of all sequences

$$x_0, x_1, \ldots, x_{n-1}$$

for all integers $n \geq 0$, where each x_i is a member of type T, is called the set (or type) of sequences of T. If $n = 0$, we have the unique *empty sequence* of T. The number of elements, n, in a sequence is called the *length* of the sequence. The index i of an element x_i within a sequence is also called a *position* in the sequence.

As mathematical objects, the finite sequences we are discussing here are not of great interest, but their computational use introduces many interesting and sometimes complex issues. The issue of insertion or deletion of elements in a sequence comes immediately to mind; the need to frequently insert or delete elements somewhere in the middle of a sequence favors a linked list representation; whereas the need to access elements in random positions, as opposed to consecutive positions, favors a vector representation.

Another discriminator between linked representations and vector representations is whether it is possible to assume a fixed upper limit on the length of sequences, in which case we refer to them as *bounded sequences*. Bounded sequences allow vector representations, whereas unbounded sequences are generally implemented as linked lists. (However, a less well-known representation called "extensible vectors" can also be used for unbounded sequences, as will be discussed in a future volume.)

We will not attempt to give a complete discussion of the tradeoffs between various linear data structures or to justify all of the assertions made in this overview or in the descriptions of the packages and subprograms given in later chapters. We have, however, tried to remain consistent with accepted terminology and notation, so that the reader can use textbooks on data structures such as [5, 8] as sources of reference in conjunction with these packages.

In the remainder of this section, we give some additional terminology for sequences that will be used in the subprogram descriptions. For a sequence S of length n, say

$$x_0, x_1, \ldots, x_{n-1}$$

we refer to x_0 as the *first* element (not the zeroth) and x_{n-1} as the *last* element.

We also commonly refer to x_0 as the left end and x_{n-1} as the right end of the sequence. Thus, if there are one or more elements $x_i, x_j, \ldots$ equal to some element x, then we refer to the element in the sequence with smallest index as the *left-most occurrence* of x in S.

In this discussion of sequences, the indices, or positions, of elements play a major role, but computationally this is not necessarily the case. When using a linked list representation, it is best to de-emphasize the calculation and use of numerical positions in favor of operations that move through sequences element by element.

2.2   Organization

2.2.1   LOW-LEVEL DATA ABSTRACTIONS

We have provided three different low-level data abstractions using singly-linked list representations:

- System_Allocated_Singly_Linked is a package that provides records containing datum and link fields, allocated using the standard heap allocation and deallocation procedures.

- The User_Allocated_Singly_Linked package provides more efficient allocation and deallocation by allocating an array of records as a storage pool, but is less flexible than the system allocated package since this array and the system heap are managed separately.

- Auto_Reallocating_Singly_Linked also uses an array of records for efficiency but automatically allocates a larger array whenever necessary; its disadvantage is that the parameters controlling the reallocation may need to be tuned to achieve optimum reallocation behavior.

These data abstractions are described in Chapters 3, 4, and 5.

2.2.2 ALGORITHMIC, STRUCTURAL AND REPRESENTATIONAL ABSTRACTIONS

The library currently includes the following algorithmic, structural and representational abstraction packages:

- **Singly_Linked_Lists** is a structural abstraction package that provides over 60 subprograms for operations on a singly-linked list representation, including numerous kinds of concatenation, deletion, substitution, searching and sorting operations.

- **Linked_List_Algorithms** is a generic algorithms package that is the source of most of the algorithms used in **Singly_Linked_Lists**; many of the algorithms will also be used in implementing the **Doubly_Linked_Lists** package.

- **Double_Ended_Lists** (described in Part 2) employs header cells with singly-linked lists to make some operations such as concatenation more efficient and to provide more security in various computations with lists.

- **Stacks** (Part 2) provides the familiar linear data structure in which insertions and deletions are restricted to one end.

- **Output_Restricted_Deques** (Part 2) provides a data structure that restricts insertions to both ends and deletions to one end.

The latter three packages are representational abstractions that produce different structural abstractions from different representations of singly-linked lists. Any of the four structural or representational abstraction packages can be plugged together with any of the three low-level data abstraction packages provided, for a total of 12 different possible combinations. Each of these 12 combinations, called a *Partially Instantiated Package*, or *PIP* for short, is included in the library. To use them one only has to instantiate the element type to a specific type. See Chapters 8 and 13 for further details on the form and usage of the PIPs.

Future additions to the library, just in the linear data structures area, may also include

- **Sequences**

- **Doubly_Linked_Lists**

- **Simple_Vectors**

- **Extensible_Vectors**

packages, along with several low-level data abstraction packages that plug together with them.

2.3   Selection from the library

There are, at a minimum, three kinds of selections to be made in using these packages:

1. the choice of a low-level data abstraction package

2. the choice of a structural or representational abstraction package

3. the choice of operations within the structural or representational package

The fact that the structure of our library allows separate choices for 1 and 2 means that there are many more selections available than would be the case with more conventional organizations. However, it is not the case that these choices are entirely independent of each other or of the choices in 3. In fact, the programmer will often have to give careful consideration to the the combination of operations that he or she expects to use in an application, and make a package selection based on algorithmic issues of time and space efficiency of the subprograms as documented in the subprogram descriptions. Another issue that might dictate a choice would be the possible exceptions raised by the operations to be used.

2.4   Package descriptions

Each package description chapter contains sections giving:

- an overview of the purpose of the data structure, the operations provided, and how they are implemented;

- the package specification (in the Ada sense), except that subprogram headers are omitted, since they appear later as part of detailed subprogram descriptions;

- the package body, with subprogram bodies omitted;

- the detailed subprogram descriptions.

A section containing a test suite for the package is also included in cases where it is meaningful.

Each subprogram description includes the subprogram header, as it would appear in the Ada package specification; some additional descriptive information and cross references; an example of use (which also forms part of the test suite for the package); and the subprogram body, with its header omitted.

The descriptive information for a subprogram includes two categories that are of special importance for data structures whose representation

involves the use of access types: **Mutative?** and **Shares?**. A subprogram
is said to be *mutative* if it changes any values in a data structure pointed
to by an access type parameter passed to the subprogram. An example
is the **Invert** function described in Chapter 6 for reversing the order of
elements in a list. **Invert** is mutative since it uses the storage cells in the
data representation of its parameter, S, to hold the result, while the related
function **Invert_Copy** leaves its parameter intact by using newly allocated
cells to hold the result. Thus after the statement

$$\text{S1 := Invert(S);}$$

the value of S may be different from its value before the statement, even
though it appears that only S1 is being affected; while

$$\text{S1 := Invert\_Copy(S);}$$

leaves the value of S unchanged. The former call is more efficient and may
be preferable if the former value of S is no longer needed. The term "de-
structive" is often applied to operations such as **Invert**, but this this terminology distorts the fact that using mutative operations can increase the
efficiency with which extensive data structure manipulations can be performed, by reusing existing storage rather than repeatedly having to allo-
cate new storage and copy the structure.

Using mutative operations does require greater care than with non-
mutative operations, particularly since storage may be *shared* among data
representations, so that a subprogram call that mutates one its parameters
may also affect the value of a variable that does not even appear in the
call. For example, sharing is established by one of the basic operations,
Construct, provided in each of the low-level data abstraction packages:
after

$$\text{S1 := Construct(X, S);}$$

all of the cells of the internal representation of S are part of the representation of S1. Thus

$$\text{S2 := Invert(S1);}$$

not only mutates S1 but also changes the value of S. Again, this will not
matter if no further use of the former value of S needs to be made.

Mutative operations and sharing are discussed further in Chapter 6.

3

System Allocated Singly Linked Package

3.1 Overview

This is the simplest of the three low-level data abstraction packages provided. It provides records containing datum and link fields, allocated using the standard heap allocation and deallocation procedures.

The exceptions that are raised by the subprograms in this package (and the other two low-level representation packages) are renamings of those defined in the package **Linked_Exceptions** (which contains nothing but exception specifications). **Linked_Exceptions** is used in a context clause of the low-level representation packages and the data abstraction packages with which they might be plugged together, so that both packages are referring to the same set of exceptions; renamings are done to make the exceptions visible outside.

3.2 Package specification

The package specification is as follows:

```
with Linked_Exceptions;
generic

   type Element is private;

package System_Allocated_Singly_Linked is

   type Sequence is private;

   Nil : constant Sequence;

   First_Of_Nil : exception
       renames Linked_Exceptions.First_Of_Nil;
   Set_First_Of_Nil : exception
       renames Linked_Exceptions.Set_First_Of_Nil;
   Next_Of_Nil : exception
       renames Linked_Exceptions.Next_Of_Nil;
   Set_Next_Of_Nil : exception
```

```
        renames Linked_Exceptions.Set_Next_Of_Nil;
  Out_Of_Construct_Storage : exception
        renames Linked_Exceptions.Out_Of_Construct_Storage;


  {The subprogram specifications}

  private

    type Node;

    type Sequence is access Node;

    Nil: constant Sequence := null;

  end System_Allocated_Singly_Linked;
```

3.3   Package body

The package body is as follows:

```
  with Unchecked_Deallocation;
  package body System_Allocated_Singly_Linked is

    type Node is record
      Datum : Element;
      Link  : Sequence;
    end record;

    procedure Free_Aux is
      new Unchecked_Deallocation(Node, Sequence);

    {The subprogram bodies}

  end System_Allocated_Singly_Linked;
```

3.4   Subprograms

3.4.1   CONSTRUCT

Specification

```
function Construct(The_Element: Element;
                   S: Sequence)
      return Sequence;
pragma inline(Construct);
```

Description   Returns the sequence whose first element is The_Element and whose following elements are those of S. S is shared.

Time   constant

Space   constant

Mutative?   No

Shares?   Yes

Details   May raise an exception, Out_Of_Construct_Storage. The relations

$$First(Construct(E,S)) = E$$
$$Next(Construct(E,S)) = S$$

always hold unless an exception is raised.

See also   First, Next, Set_First, Set_Next

Implementation

```
begin
  return new Node'(The_Element, S);
exception
  when Storage_Error =>
    raise Out_Of_Construct_Storage;
end Construct;
```

3.4.2   FIRST

Specification

```
function First(S : Sequence)
        return Element;
pragma inline(First);
```

Description   Returns the first element of S

Time   constant

Space   0

Mutative?   No

Shares?   No

Details   Raises an exception, First_Of_Nil, if $S = $ Nil.

See also   Set_First, Next

Implementation

```
begin
  return S.Datum;
exception
  when Constraint_Error =>
    raise First_Of_Nil;
end First;
```

3.4.3 FREE

Specification

```
procedure Free(S : Sequence);
pragma inline(Free);
```

Description   Causes the first cell of S to be made available for reuse. S is destroyed.

Time   constant

Space   0 (makes space available)

where $n = \text{length}(S)$

Mutative?   Yes

Shares?   No

See also

Implementation

```
   Temp : Sequence := S;
begin
   Free_Aux(Temp);
end Free;
```

3.4.4   NEXT

Specification

```
function Next(S : Sequence)
      return Sequence;
pragma inline(Next);
```

Description   Returns the sequence consisting of all the elements of S, except the first. S is shared.

Time   constant

Space   0

Mutative?   No

Shares?   Yes

Details   Raises an exception, Next_Of_Nil, if S is Nil.

See also   First, Set_Next

Implementation

```
begin
  return S.Link;
exception
  when Constraint_Error =>
    raise Next_Of_Nil;
end Next;
```

3.4.5 SET_FIRST

Specification

```
procedure Set_First(S : Sequence; X : Element);
pragma inline(Set_First);
```

Description   Changes S so that its first element is X but the following elements are unchanged.

Time   constant

Space   0

Mutative?   Yes

Shares?   No

Details   Raises an exception, Set_First_Of_Nil, if S is Nil.

See also   First, Set_Next

Implementation

```
begin
  S.Datum := X;
exception
  when Constraint_Error =>
    raise Set_First_Of_Nil;
end Set_First;
```

3.4.6   SET_NEXT

Specification

```
procedure Set_Next(S1, S2 : Sequence);
pragma inline(Set_Next);
```

Description   Changes S1 so that its first element is unchanged but the following elements are those of S2. S2 is shared.

Time   constant

Space   0

Mutative?   Yes

Shares?   Yes

Details   Raises an exception, Set_Next_Of_Nil, if S1 is Nil.

See also   Next, Set_First

Implementation

```
begin
  S1.Link := S2;
exception
  when Constraint_Error =>
    raise Set_Next_Of_Nil;
end Set_Next;
```

4

User Allocated Singly Linked Package

4.1 Overview

Compared to the System_Allocated_Singly_Linked low-level data abstraction, this package provides more efficient allocation and deallocation of list nodes by allocating an array of records as a storage pool. This however makes it less flexible than the system allocated package since the array and the system heap are managed separately, producing a greater possibility of running out of storage.

See the discussion of exceptions in Section 3.1, which applies here also.

The subprogram descriptions are identical to those for System_Allocated_Singly_Linked in all respects except the implementations.

4.2 Package specification

The package specification is as follows:

```
with Linked_Exceptions;
generic
  Heap_Size : in Natural;
  type Element is private;

package User_Allocated_Singly_Linked is

  type Sequence is private;

  Nil : constant Sequence;

  First_Of_Nil : exception
      renames Linked_Exceptions.First_Of_Nil;
  Set_First_Of_Nil : exception
      renames Linked_Exceptions.Set_First_Of_Nil;
  Next_Of_Nil : exception
      renames Linked_Exceptions.Next_Of_Nil;
  Set_Next_Of_Nil : exception
      renames Linked_Exceptions.Set_Next_Of_Nil;
  Out_Of_Construct_Storage : exception
```

```
        renames Linked_Exceptions.Out_Of_Construct_Storage;


  {The subprogram specifications}

  private

    type Sequence is new Natural;

    Nil: constant Sequence := 0;

  end User_Allocated_Singly_Linked;
```

4.3 Package body

The package body is as follows:

```
  package body User_Allocated_Singly_Linked is

    type Node is record
      Datum : Element;
      Link  : Sequence;
    end record;

    type Heap_Of_Records is array(Sequence range <>) of Node;

    Heap         : Heap_Of_Records(1 .. Sequence(Heap_Size));

    Free_List    : Sequence := Nil;

    Fill_Pointer : Sequence := 1;

  {The subprogram bodies}

  end User_Allocated_Singly_Linked;
```

4.4   Subprograms

4.4.1   CONSTRUCT

Specification

```
function Construct(The_Element : Element; S : Sequence)
      return Sequence;
pragma inline(Construct);
```

Description   Returns the sequence whose first element is The_Element and whose following elements are those of S. S is shared.

Time   constant

Space   constant

Mutative?   No

Shares?   Yes

Details   May raise an exception, Out_Of_Construct_Storage. The relations

$$\text{First}(\text{Construct}(E,S)) = E$$
$$\text{Next}(\text{Construct}(E,S)) = S$$

always hold unless an exception is raised.

See also   First, Next, Set_First, Set_Next

Implementation

```
   Temp : Sequence;
 begin
   if Free_List /= Nil then
     Temp := Free_List;
     Free_List := Next(Free_List);
   elsif Fill_Pointer <= Sequence(Heap_Size) then
     Temp := Fill_Pointer;
     Fill_Pointer := Fill_Pointer + 1;
   else
     raise Out_Of_Construct_Storage;
   end if;
   Set_First(Temp, The_Element);
   Set_Next(Temp, S);
   return (Temp);
 end Construct;
```

4.4.2   FIRST

Specification

```
function First(S : Sequence)
       return Element;
pragma inline(First);
```

Description   Returns the first element of S

Time   constant

Space   0

Mutative?   No

Shares?   No

Details   Raises an exception, First_Of_Nil, if S = Nil.

See also   Set_First, Next

Implementation

```
begin
  return Heap(S).Datum;
exception
  when Constraint_Error =>
    raise First_Of_Nil;
end First;
```

4.4.3 FREE

Specification

```
procedure Free(S : Sequence);
pragma inline(Free);
```

Description   Causes the first cell of S to be made available for reuse. S is destroyed.

Time   constant

Space   0 (makes space available)

where $n = \text{length}(S)$

Mutative?   Yes

Shares?   No

See also

Implementation

```
begin
  Set_Next(S, Free_List);
  Free_List := S;
end Free;
```

4.4.4 NEXT

Specification

```
function Next(S : Sequence)
        return Sequence;
pragma inline(Next);
```

Description   Returns the sequence consisting of all the elements of S, except the first. S is shared.

Time   constant

Space   0

Mutative?   No

Shares?   Yes

Details   Raises an exception, Next_Of_Nil, if S is Nil.

See also   First, Set_Next

Implementation

```
begin
  return Heap(S).Link;
exception
  when Constraint_Error =>
    raise Next_Of_Nil;
end Next;
```

4.4.5 SET_FIRST

Specification

```
procedure Set_First(S : Sequence; X : Element);
pragma inline(Set_First);
```

Description   Changes S so that its first element is X but the following elements are unchanged.

Time   constant

Space   0

Mutative?   Yes

Shares?   No

Details   Raises an exception, Set_First_Of_Nil, if S is Nil.

See also   First, Set_Next

Implementation

```
begin
  Heap(S).Datum := X;
exception
  when Constraint_Error =>
    raise Set_First_Of_Nil;
end Set_First;
```

4.4.6 SET_NEXT

Specification

```
procedure Set_Next(S1, S2 : Sequence);
pragma inline(Set_Next);
```

Description   Changes S1 so that its first element is unchanged but the following elements are those of S2. S2 is shared.

Time   constant

Space   0

Mutative?   Yes

Shares?   Yes

Details   Raises an exception, Set_Next_Of_Nil, if S1 is Nil.

See also   Next, Set_First

Implementation

```
begin
  Heap(S1).Link := S2;
exception
  when Constraint_Error =>
    raise Set_Next_Of_Nil;
end Set_Next;
```

5

Auto-Reallocating Singly Linked Package

5.1 Overview

Compared to the **System_Allocated_Singly_Linked** low-level data abstraction, this package provides more efficient allocation and deallocation of list nodes by allocating an array of records as a storage pool. It is also more flexible than the **User_Allocated_Singly_Linked** data abstraction, since it automatically reallocates a larger array whenever necessary. A disadvantage is that it may be necessary to tune the parameters controlling the reallocation based on characteristics of a particular application.

See the discussion of exceptions in Section 3.1, which applies here also.

The subprogram descriptions are identical to those for **System_Allocated_Singly_Linked** in all respects except the implementations.

5.2 Package specification

The package specification is as follows:

```
with Linked_Exceptions;
generic
  Initial_Number_Of_Blocks : in Positive;
  Block_Size                : in Positive;
  Coefficient               : in Float;
  type Element is private;

package Auto_Reallocating_Singly_Linked is

  type Sequence is private;

  Nil : constant Sequence;

  First_Of_Nil : exception
      renames Linked_Exceptions.First_Of_Nil;
  Set_First_Of_Nil : exception
      renames Linked_Exceptions.Set_First_Of_Nil;
  Next_Of_Nil : exception
      renames Linked_Exceptions.Next_Of_Nil;
```

```
Set_Next_Of_Nil : exception
    renames Linked_Exceptions.Set_Next_Of_Nil;
Out_Of_Construct_Storage : exception
    renames Linked_Exceptions.Out_Of_Construct_Storage;


{The subprogram specifications}

private

  type Sequence is new Natural;

  Nil: constant Sequence := 0;

end Auto_Reallocating_Singly_Linked;
```

5.3 Package body

The package body is as follows:

```
with Unchecked_Deallocation;
package body Auto_Reallocating_Singly_Linked is

  Number_Of_Blocks: Positive := Initial_Number_Of_Blocks;

  Heap_Size: Sequence :=
      Sequence(Number_Of_Blocks * Block_Size);

  type Node is record
    Datum : Element;
    Link  : Sequence;
  end record;

  type Vector_Of_Nodes is array(Sequence range <>) of Node;

  type Heap_Of_Nodes   is access Vector_Of_Nodes;

  procedure Free_Heap is
      new Unchecked_Deallocation(Vector_Of_Nodes,
                                 Heap_Of_Nodes);

  Heap        : Heap_Of_Nodes;

  Free_List   : Sequence := Nil;
```

```
Fill_Pointer : Sequence := 1;

procedure Reallocate is
  New_Number_Of_Blocks : Natural        :=
      Positive(Float(Number_Of_Blocks) * Coefficient
          + 0.5);
  New_Heap_Size         : Sequence       :=
      Sequence(New_Number_Of_Blocks * Block_Size);
  New_Heap             : Heap_Of_Nodes :=
   new Vector_Of_Nodes(1 .. New_Heap_Size);
begin
  for I in Heap'range loop
    New_Heap(I) := Heap(I);
  end loop;
  Free_Heap(Heap);
  Heap := New_Heap;
  Number_Of_Blocks := New_Number_Of_Blocks;
  Heap_Size := New_Heap_Size;
end Reallocate;


{The subprogram bodies}

begin

  Heap := new Vector_Of_Nodes(1 .. Heap_Size);

exception

  when Storage_Error =>
    raise Out_Of_Construct_Storage;

end Auto_Reallocating_Singly_Linked;
```

5.4 Subprograms

5.4.1 CONSTRUCT

Specification

```
function Construct(The_Element : Element; S : Sequence)
      return Sequence;
pragma inline(Construct);
```

Description   Returns the sequence whose first element is The_Element and whose following elements are those of S. S is shared.

Time   constant except when reallocation is necessary; in that case the time is linear in the total number of storage cells allocated.

Space   constant

Mutative?   No

Shares?   Yes

Details   May raise an exception, Out_Of_Construct_Storage. The relations

$$First(Construct(E,S)) = E$$
$$Next(Construct(E,S)) = S$$

always hold unless an exception is raised.

See also   First, Next, Set_First, Set_Next

Implementation

```
  Temp : Sequence;
begin
  if Free_List /= Nil then
    Temp := Free_List;
    Free_List := Next(Free_List);
  else
    if Fill_Pointer > Sequence(Heap_Size) then
      Reallocate;
    end if;
    Temp := Fill_Pointer;
    Fill_Pointer := Fill_Pointer + 1;
  end if;
  Set_First(Temp, The_Element);
  Set_Next(Temp, S);
  return (Temp);
end Construct;
```

5.4.2 FIRST

Specification

```
function First(S : Sequence)
       return Element;
pragma inline(First);
```

Description   Returns the first element of S

Time   constant

Space   0

Mutative?   No

Shares?   No

Details   Raises an exception, First_Of_Nil, if S = Nil.

See also   Set_First, Next

Implementation

```
begin
  return Heap(S).Datum;
exception
  when Constraint_Error =>
    raise First_Of_Nil;
end First;
```

5.4.3 FREE

Specification

```
procedure Free(S : Sequence);
pragma inline(Free);
```

Description   Causes the first cell of S to be made available for reuse. S is destroyed.

Time   constant

Space   0 (makes space available)

> **where** $n = \text{length}(S)$

Mutative?   Yes

Shares?   No

See also

Implementation

```
begin
  Set_Next(S, Free_List);
  Free_List := S;
end Free;
```

5.4.4   NEXT

Specification

```
function Next(S : Sequence)
       return Sequence;
pragma inline(Next);
```

Description   Returns the sequence consisting of all the elements of S, except the first. S is shared.

Time   constant

Space   0

Mutative?   No

Shares?   Yes

Details   Raises an exception, Next_Of_Nil, if S is Nil.

See also   First, Set_Next

Implementation

```
begin
  return Heap(S).Link;
exception
  when Constraint_Error =>
    raise Next_Of_Nil;
end Next;
```

5.4.5   SET_FIRST

Specification

```
procedure Set_First(S : Sequence; X : Element);
pragma inline(Set_First);
```

Description   Changes S so that its first element is X but the following elements are unchanged.

Time   constant

Space   0

Mutative?   Yes

Shares?   No

Details   Raises an exception, Set_First_Of_Nil, if S is Nil.

See also   First, Set_Next

Implementation

```
begin
  Heap(S).Datum := X;
exception
  when Constraint_Error =>
    raise Set_First_Of_Nil;
end Set_First;
```

5.4.6 SET_NEXT

Specification

```
procedure Set_Next(S1, S2 : Sequence);
pragma inline(Set_Next);
```

Description   Changes S1 so that its first element is unchanged but the following elements are those of S2. S2 is shared.

Time   constant

Space   0

Mutative?   Yes

Shares?   Yes

Details   Raises an exception, Set_Next_Of_Nil, if S1 is Nil.

See also   Next, Set_First

Implementation

```
begin
  Heap(S1).Link := S2;
exception
  when Constraint_Error =>
    raise Set_Next_Of_Nil;
end Set_Next;
```

6

Singly Linked Lists Package

6.1 Overview

This package provides 66 subprograms (including those that are generic formal parameters) for manipulating a singly-linked-list representation of sequences, in which the elements are of any type (supplied by a generic parameter). The purposes of these subprograms may be classified into the following three categories:

1. Construction and modification of sequences

2. Examining sequences

3. Computing with sequences

In this section we give a brief overview of these categories, leaving the details and examples of usage to the individual subprogram descriptions.

The selection of operations in this package and many details of their behavior were inspired by the sequence and list operations defined for the Common Lisp language in [9].

6.1.1 CONSTRUCTION AND MODIFICATION OF SEQUENCES

Basic construction

The most basic operation is `Construct`, which is actually a generic formal parameter to the package and is therefore supplied by another package (such as `System_Allocated_Singly_Linked`). It is assumed that `Construct` takes an element `E` and a sequence `S` and produces a new sequence whose elements are `E` followed by all the elements of `S`. By using the constant `Nil`, which is also a generic formal and represents the empty sequence, and calls to `Construct`, one can obtain particular sequences; e.g., assuming the element type is `Integer`, the expression

```
Construct(1,Construct(3,Construct(5,Nil)))
```

produces a sequence of the first three odd numbers.

The `Make_Sequence` function, given an integer `N` and an element `E`, produces a sequence of `N` elements all equal to `E`.

`Copy_Sequence(S)` returns a sequence containing the same elements as `S`, but using new cells. `Copy_First_N(S,N)` produces a sequence consisting of the first `N` elements of `S`, using new cells.

Basic modification

All of the subprograms for basic modification of sequences are procedures. Set_First(S,E) changes S so that its first element is E but the following elements are unchanged. Similarly, Set_Next(S1,S2) changes S1 so that it retains its first element but the following elements are all the elements of S2. S2 is unchanged, but the issue of argument *sharing* comes into play here. S2 is shared in the sense that the cells making it up are used also in the representation of S1. Thus if S2 is referred to later, one must remember that any change to S1 may also change S2, and vice versa.

Set_Nth(S,N,E) is a more general version of Set_First allowing change of an element in an arbitrary position. Note however that its execution time is a linear function of N, rather than constant as in the case of vector accesses. Linked list representations are most appropriate when the computation can be arranged so that operations like Set_Nth(S,N,E) that reference arbitrary positions in the list are only rarely if ever used.

There are two procedures for returning cells to the available space pool: Free(S) returns just the first cell of S, while Free_Sequence(S) returns all cells of S. Note that Set_Next(S1,S2) does not free any cells; however, it is almost always applied when S1 is the tail of a sequence, hence no cells need to be freed.

Set_First, Set_Next, and Free are actually generic parameters of the package, hence these descriptions should be regarded as requirements on these parameters.

Reversing

There are two functions for computing the reverse of a given sequence, Invert and Invert_Copy. The difference between them illustrates an important distinction that appears in numerous other pairs of operations in this package: we say that Invert(S) *mutates* its argument S, since it uses the cells of S to hold the result, while Invert_Copy leaves S intact by using newly allocated cells to hold the result. One way to implement Invert_-Copy(S) would simply be

$$\text{Invert(Copy\_Sequence(S))}$$

but the actual implementation is more efficient. (It might in fact be reasonable to implement Copy_Sequence(S) as

$$\text{Invert(Invert\_Copy(S))}$$

although a different implementation is actually used.)

Mutative operations, such as Invert and many of the operations described below, must be used with care since they can introduce subtle bugs, but they are essential to some kinds of uses of sequences, such as data base applications, and their use in other cases can mean enormous improvements in efficiency. (See also the discussion at the end of Chapter 2.)

In some cases, no non-mutative version of an operation is supplied; when it is necessary to perform such an operation on an argument that should not be mutated, one should first copy the argument; e.g., Sort, described below, is mutative and there is no Sort_Copy, so one should write

$$\texttt{Sort(Copy\_Sequence(S))}$$

if S will be needed later. The reason for not including Sort_Copy is simply that we do not know a more efficient algorithm than Sort(Copy_-Sequence(S)).

Concatenation

In a similar way, the two functions Concatenate and Concatenate_Copy provide for concatenating two sequences with or without mutating their arguments. More precisely, Concatenate(S1,S2) mutates S1 and shares S2, while Concatenate_Copy(S1,S2) builds its result out of completely new cells, leaving both S1 and S2 intact for further use.

There is another concatenation function, Append(S1,S2), which is equivalent to

$$\texttt{Concatenate(Copy\_Sequence(S1),S2)}$$

i.e., S1 is left intact and S2 is shared. The implementation is however slightly more efficient.

There are two functions which combine the functions of reversing and concatenation. Reverse_Append(S1,S2) produces a sequence containing all the elements of S1, in reverse order, followed by those of S2, in order, with S1 left intact and S2 shared. Reverse_Concatenate(S1,S2) returns the same result, but mutating S1 and sharing S2.

Merging and sorting

Merge(S1,S2) merges its arguments into a single sequence, using its generic parameter Test to compare two elements; e.g., Test might be "<=" or "<". If S1 and S2 are in order as determined by Test, then the result will be in order as determined by Test (see Section 6.1.7 for further discussion of ordering). S1 and S2 are both mutated.

If either S1 or either S2 is not in order, Merge(S1,S2) will not be in order, but it nevertheless will be an *interleaving* of S1 and S2: if element X precedes element Y in S1 then X will precede Y in Merge(S1,S2), and similarly for X and Y in S2.

Sort(S) takes a comparison function Test and returns a sequence containing the same elements as S, but in order as determined by Test; S is mutated.

Both Merge and Sort are *stable*: elements considered equal by Test (see the discussion in 6.1.7) will remain in their original relative order.

Deletion and substitution

There are eight different operations for deleting elements from a sequence, all of which have a generic parameter **Test(X)** or **Test(X,Y)**, which are **Boolean** valued functions on element values **X** and **Y**. For example, **Delete_-If(S)** returns a sequence consisting of the elements **E** of **S** except those satisfying **Test(E) = True**, mutating **S**. **Delete_Copy_If(S)** does the same thing while leaving **S** intact. See also **Delete**, **Delete_If_Not**, **Delete_-Duplicates**, and the corresponding **Copy** versions.

Similarly, there are six generic subprograms for substituting a new element for some of the elements in a sequence: **Substitute(New_Item, Old_-Item, S)**, **Substitute_If(New_Item, S)**, **Substitute_If_Not(New_Item, S)**, and the corresponding **Copy** versions.

6.1.2   EXAMINING SEQUENCES

Basic queries

Is_End(S) returns the **Boolean** value **True** if **S = Nil**, **False** otherwise. **Is_Not_End(S)** is the same as **not Is_End(S)**; it is provided purely for convenience. **Length(S)** returns the number of elements in **S**.

Counting

The remaining operations for examining sequences are generic, all having either **Test(X)** or **Test(X,Y)** as a generic parameter. For example, **Count**, **Count_If**, and **Count_If_Not** are **Integer** valued functions for counting the elements in a sequence satisfying or not satisfying **Test**.

Equality and matching

Equal(S1,S2) returns true if **S1** and **S2** contain the same elements in the same order, using **Test** as the test for the element equality. Using **"="** for **Test** one obtains the ordinary check for equality of two sequences, but this function can be used to extend other equivalence relations on elements to an equivalence relation on sequences.

A more general operation is the procedure **Mismatch**, which scans its two inputs in parallel until the first position is found at which they disagree, again using **Test** as the test for element equality. **Mismatch** sets its two output parameters to be the subsequences of its inputs beginning at the disagreement position and going to the end. **S1** and **S2** are shared. (One use of **Mismatch** is to implement **Equal**.)

Searching

There are a number of functions for searching a sequence. If **S** contains an element **E** such that **Test(Item,E)** is true, then **Find(Item,S)** returns the sequence containing the elements of **S** beginning with the leftmost such

element; otherwise **Nil** is returned. S is shared. **Find_If** and **Find_If_Not**
are related functions. **Position**, **Position_If**, and **Position_If_Not** are
similar, but return as an integer the position of the leftmost occurrence
of **Item** satisfying **Test**, or **-1** if there is none. **Search(S1,S2)** returns
leftmost occurrence in **S2** of a subsequence that element-wise matches **S1**,
using **Test** as the test for element-wise equality; **Nil** is returned if there is
no match.

The other operations for searching are all **Boolean** valued. **Some(S)** returns **True** if **Test** is true of some element of S, false otherwise. Similarly,
Every(S) checks if **Test** is true of every element of S, **Not_Every(S)** checks
if **Test** is false for some element, and **Not_Any(S)** checks if **Test** is false for
every element. All of these operations start with elements indexed $0, 1, \ldots$
and stop performing **Test** after the first element that determines the answer (e.g., if S is a sequence of integers 2, 3, 5, 7, 11, the operation is **Some**,
and **Test(X)** checks for **X** being odd, then **Test** is performed only on 2 and
3).

6.1.3   COMPUTING WITH SEQUENCES

Procedural iteration

The functions and procedures in this category are generic subprograms
for iterating over a sequence, applying some given subprogram to each element. **For_Each**, for example, is a procedure that takes a generic parameter
called **The_Procedure**; **For_Each(S)** computes **The_Procedure(E)** for each
element E of S. **For_Each_2** takes two sequences and a procedure with two
arguments and applies the procedure to corresponding pairs of elements in
the sequences.

Mapping

Map(S) applies its generic argument **F** to each element of S and returns
the results as a sequence. **F** must be a function from the **Element** type to
the **Element** type. **Map** mutates S, while **Map_Copy** leaves it intact. **Map_2**
and **Map_Copy_2** are similar functions for application of a function F of two
arguments to corresponding pairs of elements of two sequences S1 and S2.

Reduction

Reduce applies a function of two arguments, **F(X,Y)**, to reduce a sequence
to a single value; for example, if F is "+", **Reduce(S)** sums up the elements
of S. It is also necessary to supply **Reduce** with an element that is the
identity for F; e.g., 0 in the case of "+" when the elements are integers.

6.1.4 EXCEPTION HANDLING

The exceptions that are raised by the subprograms in this package are renamings of those defined in the package Linked_Exceptions; see the discussion in Section 3.1.

With all the subprograms that have subprograms as generic formal parameters, such as Test or The_Procedure, there is a question of what happens when an unhandled exception is raised by the actual subprogram to which the parameter is instantiated. In all cases, such an exception would end the processing being performed; e.g., with procedure For_Each, if an unhandled exception is raised during execution of The_Procedure on some cell X in S, the following cells are not processed.

6.1.5 NOTES ON EFFICIENCY

All of the subprograms in this package have either constant or linear time and space efficiency, with the exception of Sort, Delete_Duplicates, and Delete_Copy_Duplicates. That is, the computing time and space required to obtain the the answer is a linear function of the length of the input(s), or is a constant. In most cases, subprograms that do not have "Copy" in their names use no space at all in the sense that no new cells are used in constructing sequences, since they reuse the cells in one or more of their arguments to represent the result. The exceptions are Construct, Make_Sequence, Append, and Reverse_Append, which do use new cells in representing all or part of the results they compute.

The computing time for Sort is order $n \log n$, where n is the length of its argument. This is the maximum as well as average and minimum time for sorting (a merge-sort algorithm is used).

In the case of Delete_Duplicates and Delete_Copy_Duplicates, the computing time is order n^2, which can be very time consuming for long lists. In certain cases a faster algorithm could be used; e.g., if the elements can be totally ordered (see Section 6.1.7) then it would be faster to sort them and then eliminate the duplicates in one pass, for a total time of order $n \log n$. This assumes that order is not important in the result. Another possibility would be to use a hashing scheme, which could produce essentially linear time behavior. Neither of these alternatives may be available, however, for cases when Test is not just an equality test; e.g., see the example given in the subprogram description, in which Test is a divisibility check.

6.1.6 IMPLEMENTATION NOTES

As most of these subprograms are implemented as instances or calls of subprograms in Linked_List_Algorithms, one should refer to that package in Chapter 7 for algorithmic details. As with the algorithms in that package, there is no use of recursion and the inline pragma plays an important role in achieving efficiency.

6.1.7 ORDERINGS FOR Merge AND Sort

A precise description of the kind of function that can be used for comparing values when using the **Merge** and **Sort** subprograms can be given in terms of the notion of a *total order relation*. The generic subprogram parameter **Test** must be either a total order relation (e.g., "<" or ">") or the negation of a total order relation (e.g., ">=" or "<=").

The requirements of a total order relation $\prec$ are:

1. For all X, Y, Z, if $X \prec Y$ and $Y \prec Z$, then $X \prec Z$ (Transitive law).

2. For all X, Y, exactly one of $X \prec Y$, $Y \prec X$, or $X = Y$ holds (Trichotomy law).

In determining whether a proposed relation satisfies the trichotomy law, it is not necessary to have a strict interpretation of "="; one can introduce a notion of equivalence and define the total order relation on the equivalence classes thus defined. Or, looked at another way, we consider X and Y to be equivalent if both $X \prec Y$ and $Y \prec X$ are false. For example, X and Y might be records that have integer values in one field and the records are compared using "<" on that field. Thus two records that have the same integer in that field would be equivalent, but might not be equal because of having different values in other fields.

If **Test** is a total order relation or the negation of a total order relation, we can define the notion of a sequence **S** being "in order as determined by **Test**" as follows: for any two elements X and Y that are not equivalent (in the sense defined above), then **Test**(X, Y) is true if and only if **X** precedes **Y** in **S** . (Thus "<" or "<=" will produce ascending order, while ">" or ">=" will produce descending order.)

6.2   Package specification

The package specification is as follows:

```
with Linked_Exceptions;
 generic

   type Element0  is private;
   type Sequence0 is private;
   Nil0 : Sequence0;
   with function First0(S : Sequence0) return Element0;
   with function Next0(S : Sequence0) return Sequence0;
   with function Construct0(E : Element0; S : Sequence0)
```

```
      return Sequence0;
  with procedure Set_First0(S : Sequence0; E : Element0);
  with procedure Set_Next0(S1, S2 : Sequence0);
  with procedure Free0(S : Sequence0);

package Singly_Linked_Lists is

  subtype Element  is  Element0;
  subtype Sequence is  Sequence0;
  Nil : Sequence renames Nil0;

  First_Of_Nil : exception
      renames Linked_Exceptions.First_Of_Nil;
  Set_First_Of_Nil : exception
      renames Linked_Exceptions.Set_First_Of_Nil;
  Next_Of_Nil : exception
      renames Linked_Exceptions.Next_Of_Nil;
  Set_Next_Of_Nil : exception
      renames Linked_Exceptions.Set_Next_Of_Nil;
  Out_Of_Construct_Storage : exception
      renames Linked_Exceptions.Out_Of_Construct_Storage;


  {The subprogram specifications}

  end Singly_Linked_Lists;
```

6.3   Package body

The package body is as follows:

```
  with Linked_List_Algorithms;
  package body Singly_Linked_Lists is

    function Copy_Cell(S1, S2 : Sequence) return Sequence is
    begin
      return Construct(First(S1), S2);
    end Copy_Cell;

    pragma Inline(Copy_Cell);

    package Algorithms is
        new Linked_List_Algorithms(Cell => Sequence,
            Next => Next, Set_Next => Set_Next,
            Is_End => Is_End, Copy_Cell => Copy_Cell);
```

```
generic
  Item : Element;
  with function Test(X, Y : Element) return Boolean;
function Make_Test(S : Sequence) return Boolean;

function Make_Test(S : Sequence) return Boolean is
begin
  return Test(Item, First(S));
end Make_Test;

pragma Inline(Make_Test);

generic
  with function Test(X : Element) return Boolean;
function Make_Test_If(S : Sequence) return Boolean;

function Make_Test_If(S : Sequence) return Boolean is
begin
  return Test(First(S));
end Make_Test_If;

pragma Inline(Make_Test_If);

generic
  with function Test(X : Element) return Boolean;
function Make_Test_If_Not(S : Sequence) return Boolean;

function Make_Test_If_Not(S : Sequence) return Boolean is
begin
  return not Test(First(S));
end Make_Test_If_Not;

pragma Inline(Make_Test_If_Not);

generic
  with function Test(X, Y : Element) return Boolean;
function Make_Test_Both(S1, S2: Sequence) return Boolean;

function Make_Test_Both(S1, S2: Sequence)
    return Boolean is
begin
  return Test(First(S1), First(S2));
end Make_Test_Both;
```

```
    pragma Inline(Make_Test_Both);

  {The subprogram bodies}


  end Singly_Linked_Lists;
```

6.4   Definitions for the examples

The following definitions are referenced in the examples included in the subprogram descriptions. (This is the skeleton of a test suite in which the examples are included.)

```
    with System_Allocated_Singly_Linked_Lists;
  package Integer_Linked_Lists is new
    System_Allocated_Singly_Linked_Lists(Integer);

    with Integer_Linked_Lists, Text_Io, Examples_Help;
  procedure Examples is
    use Integer_Linked_Lists.Inner, Text_Io, Examples_Help;
    Flag : Boolean := True;   -- used in Shuffle_Test

    function Shuffle_Test(X, Y : Integer) return Boolean is
      -- used in examples of Sort and Merge subprograms to
      -- produce merge with every-other-one interleaving;
      -- ignores X and Y
    begin
      Flag := not Flag;
      return Flag;
    end Shuffle_Test;

    function Iota(N : Integer) return Sequence is
      -- returns a sequence of the integers 0,1,...,N-1
      Result : Sequence := Nil;
    begin
      for I in reverse 0 .. N - 1 loop
        Result := Construct(I, Result);
      end loop;
      return Result;
    end Iota;

    procedure Show_List(S : Sequence) is
      -- prints the sequence S on a line beginning with --:
      -- using Print_Integer from Examples_Help
      procedure Show_List_Aux is new For_Each(Print_Integer);
```

```
  begin
    Put("--:"); Show_List_Aux(S); New_Line;
  end Show_List;

begin


 {Examples from the subprograms}


 end Examples;
```

6.5   Subprograms

6.5.1   APPEND

Specification

```
function Append(S1, S2 : Sequence)
       return Sequence;
```

Description   Returns a sequence containing all the elements of S1 followed by those of S2. S2 is shared.

Time   order n_1

Space   order n_1

  where $n_1 = \text{length}(S1)$

Mutative?   No

Shares?   Yes

See also   Concatenate, Concatenate_Copy

Examples

```
Show_List(Append(Iota(5), Iota(6)));
--   0  1  2  3  4  0  1  2  3  4  5
Show_List(Append(Nil, Iota(6)));
--   0  1  2  3  4  5
Show_List(Append(Iota(5), Nil));
--   0  1  2  3  4
```

Implementation

```
begin
  return Algorithms.Append(S1, S2);
end Append;
```

6.5.2 BUTLAST

Specification

```
function Butlast(S : Sequence; N : Integer := 1)
       return Sequence;
```

Description   Returns a sequence containing all of the elements of S except the last N elements. S is mutated.

Time   order n

Space   0

where $n = \text{length}(S)$

Mutative?   Yes

Shares?   No

See also   Butlast_Copy, Subseqeunce

Examples

```
Show_List(Butlast(Iota(5)));
--  0  1  2  3
Show_List(Butlast(Iota(5), 3));
--  0  1
Show_List(Butlast(Iota(5), 5));
--
```

Implementation

```
   I : Integer := Length(S) - N;
begin
   if I <= 0 then
     return Nil;
   elsif N > 0 then
     Set_Next(Nth_Rest(I - 1, S), Nil);
   end if;
   return S;
end Butlast;
```

6.5.3 BUTLAST_COPY

Specification

```
function Butlast_Copy(S : Sequence; N : Integer := 1)
      return Sequence;
```

Description   Returns a sequence containing all of the elements of S except the last N elements.

Time   order n

Space $n - N$

   where $n = \text{length}(S)$

Mutative?   No

Shares?   No

See also   Butlast, Subsequence

Examples

```
Show_List(Butlast_Copy(Iota(5)));
--  0  1  2  3
Show_List(Butlast_Copy(Iota(5), 3));
--  0  1
Show_List(Butlast_Copy(Iota(5), 5));
--
```

Implementation

```
begin
  return Copy_First_N(S, Length(S) - N);
end Butlast_Copy;
```

6.5.4 CONCATENATE

Specification

```
function Concatenate(S1, S2 : Sequence)
         return Sequence;
```

Description   Returns a sequence containing all the elements of S1 followed by those of S2. S1 is mutated and S2 is shared.

Time   order n_1

Space   0

    where $n_1 = \text{length(S1)}$

Mutative?   Yes

Shares?   Yes

See also   Append, Concatenate_Copy

Examples

```
Show_List(Concatenate(Iota(5), Iota(6)));
--  0  1  2  3  4  0  1  2  3  4  5
Show_List(Concatenate(Nil, Iota(6)));
--  0  1  2  3  4  5
Show_List(Concatenate(Iota(5), Nil));
--  0  1  2  3  4
```

Implementation

```
begin
  if Is_End(S1) then
    return S2;
  end if;
  Set_Next(Last(S1), S2);
  return S1;
end Concatenate;
```

6.5.5   CONCATENATE_COPY

Specification

```
function Concatenate_Copy(S1, S2 : Sequence)
       return Sequence;
```

Description   Returns a sequence containing all the elements of S1 followed by those of S2.

Time   order $n_1 + n_2$

Space   order $n_1 + n_2$

    where $n_1 = \text{length}(S1)$ and $n_2 = \text{length}(S2)$

Mutative?   No

Shares?   No

See also   Append, Concatenate

Implementation

```
begin
  return Append(S1, Append(S2, Nil));
end Concatenate_Copy;
```

6.5.6 CONSTRUCT

Specification

```
function Construct(E: Element; S : Sequence)
        return Sequence renames Construct0;
```

Description   Returns the sequence whose first element is E and whose following elements are those of S. S is shared.

Time   constant

Space   constant

Mutative?   No

Shares?   Yes

Details   This description is actually a requirement on Construct0, a generic formal parameter of the package. May raise an exception, Out_-Of_Construct_Storage. The relations

$$First(Construct(E,S)) = E$$
$$Next(Construct(E,S)) = S$$

always hold unless an exception is raised.

See also   First, Next, Set_First, Set_Next

6.5.7   COPY_FIRST_N

Specification

```
function Copy_First_N(S : Sequence; N : Integer)
      return Sequence;
```

Description   Returns a copy of the first N elements of S.

Time   order N

Space   order N

Mutative?   No

Shares?   No

See also   Butlast, Butlast_Copy, Copy_Sequence

Implementation

```
begin
  return Algorithms.Append_First_N(S, Nil, N);
end Copy_First_N;
```

6.5.8 COPY_SEQUENCE

Specification

```
function Copy_Sequence(S : Sequence)
      return Sequence;
```

Description   Returns a sequence containing the same elements as S, in the same order, but using separate storage cells.

Time   order n

Space   order n

  where $n = \text{length}(S)$

Mutative?   No

Shares?   No

See also   Butlast, Butlast_Copy, Copy_First_N

Implementation

```
begin
  return Append(S, Nil);
end Copy_Sequence;
```

6.5.9 COUNT

Specification

```
generic
with function Test(X, Y : Element) return Boolean;
function Count(Item : Element; S : Sequence)
        return Integer;
```

Description   Returns a non-negative integer equal to the number of elements E of S such that Test(Item,E) is true.

Time   order nm

Space   0

>   **where** $n =$ length(S)and m is the average time for Test

Mutative?   No

Shares?   No

See also   Count_If, Count_If_Not, Find

Examples

```
declare
  function Count_When_Divides is
    new Integer_Linked_Lists.Inner.Count(Test => Divides);
begin
  Show_Integer(Count_When_Divides(3, Iota(10)));
--   4
end;
```

Implementation

```
   function Test_Aux is new Make_Test(Item, Test);
   function Count_Aux is new Algorithms.Count(Test_Aux);
begin
  return Count_Aux(S);
end Count;
```

6.5.10   COUNT_IF

Specification

```
generic
with function Test(X : Element) return Boolean;
function Count_If(S : Sequence)
        return Integer;
```

Description   Returns a non-negative integer equal to the number of elements E of S such that Test(E) is true.

Time   order nm

Space   0

>   where $n = $ length(S)and m is the average time for Test

Mutative?   No

Shares?   No

See also   Count, Count_If_Not, Find, Find_If

Examples

```
declare
   function Count_If_Odd is new Count_If(Test => Odd);
begin
   Show_Integer(Count_If_Odd(Iota(9)));
-- 4
end;
```

Implementation

```
   function Test_Aux is new Make_Test_If(Test);
   function Count_Aux is new Algorithms.Count(Test_Aux);
begin
   return Count_Aux(S);
end Count_If;
```

6.5.11   COUNT_IF_NOT

Specification

```
generic
with function Test(X : Element) return Boolean;
function Count_If_Not(S : Sequence)
        return Integer;
```

Description   Returns a non-negative integer equal to the number of elements E of S such that Test(E) is false.

Time   order nm

Space   0

> where $n = $ length(S) and m is the average time for Test

Mutative?   No

Shares?   No

See also   Count, Count_If, Find, Find_If_Not

Examples

```
declare
   function Count_If_Not_Odd is
        new Count_If_Not(Test => Odd);
 begin
   Show_Integer(Count_If_Not_Odd(Iota(9)));
-- 5
 end;
```

Implementation

```
   function Test_Aux is new Make_Test_If_Not(Test);
   function Count_Aux is new Algorithms.Count(Test_Aux);
 begin
   return Count_Aux(S);
 end Count_If_Not;
```

6.5.12 DELETE

Specification

```
generic
with function Test(X, Y : Element) return Boolean;
function Delete(Item : Element; S : Sequence)
        return Sequence;
```

Description   Returns a sequence consisting of all the elements E of S except those for which Test(Item,E) is true. S is mutated.

Time   order nm

Space   0

   where $n = $ length(S)and m is the average time for Test

Mutative?   Yes

Shares?   No

See also   Delete_If, Delete_If_Not

Examples

```
declare
    function Delete_When_Divides is new
        Integer_Linked_Lists.Inner.Delete(Test => Divides);
begin
   Show_List(Delete_When_Divides(3, Iota(15)));
-- 1  2  4  5  7  8  10  11  13  14
end;
```

Implementation

```
   function Test_Aux is new Make_Test(Item, Test);
   procedure Partition_Aux
     is new Algorithms.Invert_Partition(Test_Aux);
   Temp_1, Temp_2: Sequence := Nil;
begin
  Partition_Aux(S, Temp_1, Temp_2);
  Free_Sequence(Temp_1);
  return Invert(Temp_2);
end Delete;
```

6.5.13   DELETE_COPY

Specification

```
generic
with function Test(X, Y : Element) return Boolean;
function Delete_Copy(Item : Element; S : Sequence)
       return Sequence;
```

Description   Returns a sequence consisting of all the elements E of S
except those for which Test(Item,E) is true.

Time   order nm

Space   order n

   where $n = $ length(S)and m is the average time for Test

Mutative?   No

Shares?   No

See also   Delete

Examples

```
declare
  function Delete_Copy_When_Divides is new
   Integer_Linked_Lists.Inner.Delete_Copy(Test => Divides);
begin
  Show_List(Delete_Copy_When_Divides(3, Iota(15)));
--   1  2  4  5  7  8  10  11  13  14
end;
```

Implementation

```
   function Test_Aux is new Make_Test(Item, Test);
   function Delete_Copy_Aux
     is new Algorithms.Delete_Copy_Append(Test_Aux);
begin
  return Delete_Copy_Aux(S, Nil);
end Delete_Copy;
```

6.5.14   DELETE_COPY_DUPLICATES

Specification

```
generic
with function Test(X, Y : Element) return Boolean;
function Delete_Copy_Duplicates(S : Sequence)
        return Sequence;
```

Description   Returns a sequence of the elements of S but with only one occurrence of each, using Test as the test for equality.

Time   order n^2m

Space   order n

where $n = $ length(S)and m is the average time for Test

Mutative?   No

Shares?   No

Details   The left-most occurrence of each duplicated item is retained.

See also   Delete_Duplicates

Examples

```
declare
   function Delete_Copy_Duplicates_When_Divides
     is new Delete_Copy_Duplicates(Test=>Divides);
begin
  Show_List(Delete_Copy_Duplicates_When_Divides(
      Next(Next(Iota(20)))));
--   2  3  5  7  11  13  17  19
end;
```

Implementation

```
   function Test_Aux is new Make_Test_Both(Test);
   function Delete_Copy_Aux
     is new Algorithms.Delete_Copy_Duplicates_Append(
         Test_Aux);
begin
  return Delete_Copy_Aux(S, Nil);
end Delete_Copy_Duplicates;
```

6.5.15   DELETE_COPY_IF

Specification

```
generic
with function Test(X : Element) return Boolean;
function Delete_Copy_If(S : Sequence)
        return Sequence;
```

Description   Returns a sequence consisting of all the elements E of S except those for which Test(E) is true.

Time   order nm

Space   order n

> **where** $n =$ length(S)and m is the average time for Test

Mutative?   No

Shares?   No

See also   Delete_If, Delete_Copy_If_Not

Examples

```
declare
  function Delete_Copy_If_Odd is new
      Delete_Copy_If(Test => Odd);
begin
  Show_List(Delete_Copy_If_Odd(Iota(10)));
--   0  2  4  6  8
end;
```

Implementation

```
    function Test_Aux is new Make_Test_If(Test);
    function Delete_Copy_Aux
      is new Algorithms.Delete_Copy_Append(Test_Aux);
begin
  return Delete_Copy_Aux(S, Nil);
end Delete_Copy_If;
```

6.5.16 DELETE_COPY_IF_NOT

Specification

```
generic
with function Test(X : Element) return Boolean;
function Delete_Copy_If_Not(S : Sequence)
        return Sequence;
```

Description   Returns a sequence consisting of all the elements E of S except those for which Test(E) is false.

Time   order nm

Space   order n

> **where** $n = $ length(S)and m is the average time for Test

Mutative?   No

Shares?   Yes

See also   Delete_If_Not, Delete_Copy_If

Examples

```
declare
    function Delete_Copy_If_Not_Odd is
        new Delete_Copy_If_Not(Test => Odd);
begin
  Show_List(Delete_Copy_If_Not_Odd(Iota(10)));
--  1  3  5  7  9
end;
```

Implementation

```
    function Test_Aux is new Make_Test_If_Not(Test);
    function Delete_Copy_Aux
      is new Algorithms.Delete_Copy_Append(Test_Aux);
begin
  return Delete_Copy_Aux(S, Nil);
end Delete_Copy_If_Not;
```

6.5.17   DELETE_DUPLICATES

Specification

```
generic
with function Test(X, Y : Element) return Boolean;
function Delete_Duplicates(S : Sequence)
        return Sequence;
```

Description   Returns a sequence of the elements of S but with only one occurrence of each, using Test as the test for equality. S is mutated.

Time   order n^2m

Space   0

> **where** $n = \text{length}(S)$ and m is the average time for Test

Mutative?   Yes

Shares?   No

Details   The left-most occurrence of each duplicated item is retained.

See also   Delete_Copy_Duplicates

Examples

```
declare
  function Delete_Duplicates_When_Divides is
      new Delete_Duplicates(Test=>Divides);
begin
  Show_List(Delete_Duplicates_When_Divides(
      Next(Next(Iota(20)))));
--  2  3  5  7  11  13  17  19
end;
```

Implementation

```
  function Test_Aux is new Make_Test_Both(Test);
  function Delete_Aux is
    new Algorithms.Delete_Duplicates(Test_Aux, Free);
begin
  return Delete_Aux(S);
end Delete_Duplicates;
```

6.5.18   DELETE_IF

Specification

```
generic
with function Test(X : Element) return Boolean;
function Delete_If(S : Sequence)
        return Sequence;
```

Description   Returns a sequence consisting of all the elements E of S except those for which Test(E) is true.

Time   order nm

Space   order n

> **where** $n =$ length(S)and m is the average time for Test

Mutative?   Yes

Shares?   No

See also   Delete_Copy_If, Delete_If_Not

Examples

```
declare
    function Delete_If_Odd is
        new Delete_If(Test => Odd);
begin
  Show_List(Delete_If_Odd(Iota(10)));
--  0  2  4  6  8
end;
```

Implementation

```
   function Test_Aux is new Make_Test_If(Test);
   procedure Partition_Aux
     is new Algorithms.Invert_Partition(Test_Aux);
   Temp_1, Temp_2: Sequence := Nil;
begin
  Partition_Aux(S, Temp_1, Temp_2);
  Free_Sequence(Temp_1);
  return Invert(Temp_2);
end Delete_If;
```

6.5.19   DELETE_IF_NOT

Specification

```
generic
with function Test(X : Element) return Boolean;
function Delete_If_Not(S : Sequence)
        return Sequence;
```

Description   Returns a sequence consisting of all the elements E of S except those for which Test(E) is false. S is mutated.

Time   order nm

Space   order n

> **where** $n = $ length(S)and m is the average time for Test

Mutative?   Yes

Shares?   No

See also   Delete_Copy_If_Not, Delete_If

Examples

```
declare
    function Delete_If_Not_Odd is
        new Delete_If_Not(Test => Odd);
begin
  Show_List(Delete_If_Not_Odd(Iota(10)));
--   1  3  5  7  9
end;
```

Implementation

```
  function Test_Aux is new Make_Test_If(Test);
  procedure Partition_Aux is
    new Algorithms.Invert_Partition(Test_Aux);
  Temp_1, Temp_2: Sequence := Nil;
begin
  Partition_Aux(S, Temp_1, Temp_2);
  Free_Sequence(Temp_2);
  return Invert(Temp_1);
end Delete_If_Not;
```

6.5.20 EQUAL

Specification

```
generic
with function Test(X, Y : Element) return Boolean;
function Equal(S1, S2 : Sequence)
       return Boolean;
```

Description   Returns true if S1 and S2 contain the same elements in the same order, using Test as the test for element equality.

Time   order $m \min(\text{length}(S1), \text{length}(S2))$

Space   0

> **where** m is the average time for Test

Mutative?   No

Shares?   No

See also   Mismatch

Examples

```
declare
    function Equal_Equal is new Equal(Test => "=");
begin
   Show_Boolean(Equal_Equal(Iota(10),Iota(10)));
--True
   Show_Boolean(Equal_Equal(Iota(10),Iota(11)));
--False
   Show_Boolean(Equal_Equal(Invert(Iota(10)),Iota(10)));
--False
   Show_Boolean(Equal_Equal(Iota(10),Nil));
--False
   Show_Boolean(Equal_Equal(Nil,Iota(10)));
--False
   Show_Boolean(Equal_Equal(Nil,Nil));
--True
end;
```

Implementation

```
   function Test_Aux is new Make_Test_Both(Test);
   function Equal_Aux is new Algorithms.Equal(Test_Aux);
begin
  return Equal_Aux(S1, S2);
end Equal;
```

6.5.21   EVERY

Specification

```
generic
with function Test(X : Element) return Boolean;
function Every(S : Sequence)
        return Boolean;
```

Description   Returns true if Test is true of every element of S, false otherwise. Elements numbered 0, 1, 2, ... are tried in order.

Time   order nm

Space   0

> **where** $n = $ length(S)and m is the average time for Test

Mutative?   No

Shares?   No

Details   Returns true if S is Nil.

See also   Not_Every, Some

Examples

```
declare
    function Every_Odd is new Every(Test => Odd);
    function Delete_If_Not_Odd is
        new Delete_If_Not(Test => Odd);
begin
  Show_Boolean(Every_Odd(Iota(10)));
--False
  Show_Boolean(Every_Odd(Delete_If_Not_Odd(Iota(10))));
--True
end;
```

Implementation

```
    function Test_Aux is new Make_Test_If(Test);
    function Every_Aux is new Algorithms.Every(Test_Aux);
begin
  return Every_Aux(S);
end Every;
```

6.5.22   FIND

Specification

```
generic
with function Test(X, Y : Element) return Boolean;
function Find(Item : Element; S : Sequence)
        return Sequence;
```

Description   If S contains an element E such that Test(Item,E) is true, then the sequence containing elements of S beginning with the leftmost such element is returned; otherwise Nil is returned.

Time   order nm

Space   0

where $n = $ length(S)and m is the average time for Test

Mutative?   No

Shares?   Yes

See also   Find_If, Find_If_Not, Some, Search

Examples

```
declare
    function Find_When_Greater is new Find(Test => "<");
begin
    Show_List(Find_When_Greater(9, Iota(20)));
--   10  11  12  13  14  15  16  17  18  19
end;
```

Implementation

```
   function Test_Aux is new Make_Test(Item, Test);
   function Find_Aux is new Algorithms.Find(Test_Aux);
begin
   return Find_Aux(S);
end Find;
```

6.5.23   FIND_IF

Specification

```
generic
with function Test(X : Element) return Boolean;
function Find_If(S : Sequence)
        return Sequence;
```

Description   If S contains an element E such that Test(E) is true, then a sequence containing the elements of S beginning with the leftmost such element is returned; otherwise Nil is returned.

Time   order nm

Space   0

>   **where** $n = \text{length}(S)$ and m is the average time for Test

Mutative?   No

Shares?   Yes

See also   Find, Find_If_Not, Some, Search

Examples

```
declare
    function Find_If_Greater_Than_7
       is new Find_If(Test => Greater_Than_7);
 begin
    Show_List(Find_If_Greater_Than_7(Iota (15)));
 --  8  9  10  11  12  13  14
 end;
```

Implementation

```
   function Test_Aux is new Make_Test_If(Test);
   function Find_Aux is new Algorithms.Find(Test_Aux);
 begin
   return Find_Aux(S);
 end Find_If;
```

6.5.24 FIND_IF_NOT

Specification

```
generic
with function Test(X : Element) return Boolean;
function Find_If_Not(S : Sequence)
        return Sequence;
```

Description   If S contains an element E such that Test(E) is false, then a sequence containing the elements of S beginning with the leftmost such element is returned; otherwise Nil is returned.

Time   order nm

Space   0

>   where $n = $ length(S)and m is the average time for Test

Mutative?   No

Shares?   Yes

See also   Find, Find_If, Some, Search

Examples

```
declare
  function Find_If_Not_Greater_Than_7
      is new Find_If_Not(Test => Greater_Than_7);
begin
  Show_List(Find_If_Not_Greater_Than_7(
      Invert(Iota (15))));
--  7  6  5  4  3  2  1  0
end;
```

Implementation

```
    function Test_Aux is new Make_Test_If_Not(Test);
    function Find_Aux is new Algorithms.Find(Test_Aux);
begin
  return Find_Aux(S);
end Find_If_Not;
```

6.5.25 FIRST

Specification

```
function First(S : Sequence)
       return Element renames First0;
```

Description   Returns the first element of S

Time   constant

Space   0

Mutative?   No

Shares?   No

Details   This description is actually a requirement on First0, a generic formal parameter of the package. Raises an exception, First_Of_Nil, if S = Nil.

See also   Set_First, Next

6.5.26   FOR_EACH

Specification

```
generic
with procedure The_Procedure(X : Element);
procedure For_Each(S : Sequence);
```

Description   Applies The_Procedure to each element of S.

Time   order np

Space   0

> **where** $n = $ length(S)and p is the average time for The_Procedure

Mutative?   No

Shares?   No

Details   S : Sequence

See also   For_Each_2, Map

Implementation

```
procedure The_Procedure_Aux(X : Sequence) is
begin
  The_Procedure(First(X));
end The_Procedure_Aux;
pragma Inline(The_Procedure_Aux);
procedure For_Each_Aux
  is new Algorithms.For_Each_Cell(The_Procedure_Aux);
begin
  For_Each_Aux(S);
end For_Each;
```

6.5.27   FOR_EACH_CELL

Specification

```
generic
with procedure The_Procedure(X : Sequence);
procedure For_Each_Cell(S : Sequence);
```

Description   Applies The_Procedure to each storage cell of S.

Time   order np

Space   0

   where $n = \text{length}(S)$ and p is the average time for The_Procedure

Mutative?   No

Shares?   No

See also   For_Each, Map

Implementation

```
   procedure For_Each_Aux
      is new Algorithms.For_Each_Cell(The_Procedure);
 begin
   For_Each_Aux(S);
 end For_Each_Cell;
```

6.5.28 FOR_EACH_2

Specification

```
generic
      with procedure The_Procedure(X, Y : Element);
   procedure For_Each_2(S1, S2 : Sequence);
```

Description   Applies The_Procedure to pairs of elements of S1 and S2 in the same position.

Time   order np

Space   order n

> **where** p is the average time for The_Procedure, $n = \min(n_1, n_2)$, $n_1 = \text{length(S1)}$, $n_2 = \text{length(S2)}$

Mutative?   No

Shares?   No

Details   Stops when the end of either S1 or S2 is reached.

See also   For_Each, For_Each_Cell_2, Map

Implementation

```
procedure The_Procedure_Aux(X, Y : Sequence) is
begin
  The_Procedure(First(X), First(Y));
end The_Procedure_Aux;
pragma Inline(The_Procedure_Aux);
procedure For_Each_Aux
   is new Algorithms.For_Each_Cell_2(The_Procedure_Aux);
begin
  For_Each_Aux(S1,S2);
end For_Each_2;
```

6.5.29   FOR_EACH_CELL_2

Specification

```
generic
      with procedure The_Procedure(X, Y : Sequence);
procedure For_Each_Cell_2(S1, S2 : Sequence);
```

Description   Applies The_Procedure to pairs of cells of S1 and S2 in the same position.

Time   order np

Space   order n

    where p is the average time for The_Procedure, $n = \min(n_1, n_2)$, $n_1 = \text{length(S1)}$, $n_2 = \text{length(S2)}$

Mutative?   No

Shares?   No

Details   Stops when the end of either S1 or S2 is reached.

See also   For_Each_Cell, For_Each_2, Map

Implementation

```
   procedure For_Each_Aux
      is new Algorithms.For_Each_Cell_2(The_Procedure);
begin
   For_Each_Aux(S1,S2);
end For_Each_Cell_2;
```

6.5.30 FREE

Specification

```
procedure Free(S : Sequence) renames Free0;
```

Description   Causes the first cell of S to be made available for reuse. S is destroyed.

Time   constant

Space   0 (makes space available)

   where $n = \text{length}(S)$

Mutative?   Yes

Shares?   No

See also   Free_Sequence

6.5.31   FREE_SEQUENCE

Specification

```
procedure Free_Sequence(S : Sequence);
```

Description   Causes the storage cells occupied by S to be made available for reuse. No further reference should be made to S or to any sequence that shares with S.

Time   order n

Space   0 (makes space available)

   where $n = \text{length(S)}$

Mutative?   Yes

Shares?   No

See also   Free

Implementation

```
   procedure Free_Sequence_Aux is
        new Algorithms.For_Each_Cell(Free);
begin
   Free_Sequence_Aux(S);
end Free_Sequence;
```

6.5.32   INVERT

Specification

```
function Invert(S : Sequence)
       return Sequence;
```

Description   Returns a sequence containing the same elements as S but in reverse order. S is mutated.

Time   order n

Space   0

>   where $n = \text{length}(S)$

Mutative?   Yes

Shares?   No

See also   Invert_Copy, Reverse_Append, Reverse_Concatenate

Examples

```
    Show_List(Invert(Iota(6)));
--   5  4  3  2  1  0
```

Implementation

```
begin
  return Reverse_Concatenate(S, Nil);
end Invert;
```

6.5.33   INVERT_COPY

Specification

```
function Invert_Copy(S : Sequence)
      return Sequence;
```

Description   Returns a new sequence containing the same elements as S but in reverse order.

Time   order n

Space   order n

   where $n = \text{length}(S)$

Mutative?   No

Shares?   No

See also   Invert, Reverse_Append, Reverse_Concatenate

Examples

```
    Show_List(Invert_Copy(Iota(6)));
--   5  4  3  2  1  0
```

Implementation

```
begin
  return Reverse_Append(S, Nil);
end Invert_Copy;
```

6.5.34   Is_END

Specification

```
function Is_End(S : Sequence)
      return Boolean;
```

Description   Returns true if S is the Nil sequence, false otherwise.

Time   constant

Space   0

Mutative?   No

Shares?   No

See also   Is_Not_End

Implementation

```
begin
  return S = Nil;
end Is_End;
```

6.5.35   Is_Not_End

Specification

```
function Is_Not_End(S : Sequence)
      return Boolean;
```

Description   Returns false if S is the Nil sequence, true otherwise.

Time   constant

Space   0

Mutative?   No

Shares?   No

See also   Is_End

Implementation

```
begin
  return not Is_End(S);
end Is_Not_End;
```

6.5.36   LAST

Specification

```
function Last(S : Sequence)
       return Sequence;
```

Description   Returns the sequence containing just the last element of S.

Time   order n

Space   0

where $n = \text{length}(S)$

Mutative?   No

Shares?   Yes

Details   Raises an exception, Next_Of_Nil, if S is Nil.

See also   First

Examples

```
    Show_List(Last(Iota(6)));
 --   5
```

Implementation

```
begin
  return Algorithms.Last(S);
end Last;
```

6.5.37 LENGTH

Specification

```
function Length(S : Sequence)
        return Integer;
```

Description   The number of elements in S is returned as a non-negative integer.

Time   order n

Space   0

>   **where** $n = \text{length}(S)$

Mutative?   No

Shares?   No

See also

Implementation

```
begin
  return Algorithms.Length(S);
end Length;
```

6.5.38 MAKE_SEQUENCE

Specification

```
function Make_Sequence(Size : Integer; Initial : Element)
       return Sequence;
```

Description   Returns a sequence of length Size in which each element has the value of Initial.

Time   order Size

Space   order Size

Mutative?   No

Shares?   No

See also

Examples

```
    Show_List(Make_Sequence(5, 9));
 --  9  9  9  9  9
```

Implementation

```
  Result : Sequence := Nil;
  I      : Integer  := Size;
begin
  while I > 0 loop
    Result := Construct(Initial, Result);
    I := I - 1;
  end loop;
  return Result;
end Make_Sequence;
```

6.5.39 MAP

Specification

```
generic
with function F(E : Element) return Element;
function Map(S : Sequence)
        return Sequence;
```

Description   Returns a sequence consisting of the results of applying F
to each element of S. S is mutated.

Time   order nf

Space   order n

> where $n = $ length(S)and f is the average time for F

Mutative?   Yes

Shares?   No

See also   Map_Copy, Map_2, For_Each

Examples

```
declare
        function Map_Square is new Map(F => Square);
begin
   Show_List(Map_Square(Iota(5)));
--   0   1   4   9   16
end;
```

Implementation

```
   procedure The_Procedure_Aux(S : Sequence) is
   begin
     Set_First(S, F(First(S)));
   end The_Procedure_Aux;
   pragma Inline(The_Procedure_Aux);
   procedure Map_Aux
     is new Algorithms.For_Each_Cell(The_Procedure_Aux);
begin
  Map_Aux(S);
   return S;
end Map;
```

6.5.40   MAP_2

Specification

```
generic
with function F(X, Y : Element) return Element;
function Map_2(S1, S2 : Sequence)
       return Sequence;
```

Description   Returns a sequence consisting of the results of applying F to corresponding elements of S1 and S2. S1 is mutated.

Time   order nf

Space   order n

> **where** f is the average time for F, $n = \min(n_1, n_2)$, $n_1 = \text{length}(S1)$, $n_2 = \text{length}(S2)$

Mutative?   Yes

Shares?   No

Details   Suppose that $X_0, X_1, \ldots, X_{n_1-1}$ are the elements of S1 and $Y_0, Y_1, \ldots, Y_{n_2-1}$ are of S2. The sequence returned by Map_2 consists of F(X_0, Y_0), F(X_1, Y_1), ..., F(X_{n-1}, Y_{n-1}), followed by $X_n, \ldots, X_{n_1-1}$ in the case that $n_1 > n_2$ (where $n = \min(n_1, n_2)$).

See also   Map, Map_Copy_2, For_Each

Examples

```
declare
        function Map_2_Times is new Map_2(F => "*");
begin
   Show_List(Map_2_Times(Iota(5), Invert(Iota(5))));
--   0  3  4  3  0
end;
```

Implementation

```
   procedure The_Procedure_Aux(S1, S2 : Sequence) is
   begin
     Set_First(S1, F(First(S1), First(S2)));
   end The_Procedure_Aux;
   pragma Inline(The_Procedure_Aux);
   procedure Map_Aux
     is new Algorithms.For_Each_Cell_2(The_Procedure_Aux);
 begin
   Map_Aux(S1, S2);
   return S1;
 end Map_2;
```

6.5.41   MAP_COPY

Specification

```
generic
with function F(E : Element) return Element;
function Map_Copy(S : Sequence)
        return Sequence;
```

Description   Returns a sequence consisting of the results of applying F to each element of S.

Time   order nf

Space   order n

> **where** $n = \text{length}(S)$ and f is the average time for F

Mutative?   No

Shares?   No

See also   Map, For_Each

Examples

```
declare
  function Map_Copy_Square is
      new Map_Copy(F => Square);
begin
  Show_List(Map_Copy_Square(Iota(5)));
--  0  1  4  9  16
end;
```

Implementation

```
    function Make_Cell(S1, S2 : Sequence) return Sequence is
    begin
      return Construct(F(First(S1)), S2);
    end Make_Cell;
    pragma Inline(Make_Cell);
    function Map_Copy_Aux
      is new Algorithms.Map_Copy_Append(Make_Cell);
  begin
    return Map_Copy_Aux(S, Nil);
  end Map_Copy;
```

6.5.42   MAP_COPY_2

Specification

```
generic
with function F(X, Y : Element) return Element;
function Map_Copy_2(S1, S2 : Sequence)
        return Sequence;
```

Description   Returns a sequence consisting of the results of applying F to corresponding elements of S1 and S2.

Time   order nf

Space   order n

> **where** f is the average time for F, $n = \min(n_1, n_2)$, $n_1 = \text{length}(S1)$, $n_2 = \text{length}(S2)$

Mutative?   No

Shares?   No

Details   Suppose that $X_0, X_1, \ldots, X_{n_1-1}$ are the elements of S1 and $Y_0, Y_1, \ldots, Y_{n_2-1}$ are those of S2. The sequence returned by Map_Copy_2 consists of the values $F(X_0, Y_0)$, $F(X_1, Y_1)$, ..., $F(X_{n-1}, Y_{n-1})$, where $n = \min(n_1, n_2)$.

See also   Map_2

Examples

```
declare
    function Map_Copy_2_Times is new Map_Copy_2(F => "*");
begin
  Show_List(Map_Copy_2_Times(Iota(5), Invert(Iota(5))));
--   0  3  4  3  0
end;
```

Implementation

```
function Make_Cell(S1, S2, S3: Sequence)
    return Sequence is
begin
  return Construct(F(First(S1), First(S2)), S3);
end Make_Cell;
pragma Inline(Make_Cell);
function Map_Copy_Aux
  is new Algorithms.Map_Copy_2_Append(Make_Cell);
begin
  return Map_Copy_Aux(S1, S2, Nil);
end Map_Copy_2;
```

6.5.43 MERGE

Specification

```
generic
with function Test(X, Y :Element) return Boolean;
function Merge(S1, S2 : Sequence)
        return Sequence;
```

Description   Returns a sequence containing the same elements as S1 and S2, interleaved. If S1 and S2 are in order as determined by Test, then the result will be also. Both S1 and S2 are mutated.

Time   order $(n_1 + n_2)m$

Space   order $n_1 + n_2$

   where $n_1 = \text{length}(S1)$, $n_2 = \text{length}(S2)$, and m is the average time for Test

Mutative?   Yes

Shares?   No

Details   By "interleaved" is meant that if X precedes Y in S1 then X will precede Y in Merge(S1, S2) and similarly for X and Y in S2 (even if S1 or S2 is not in order). The property of stability also holds. See Section 6.1.7 for discussion of the restrictions on Test and definition of "in order as determined by Test."

See also   Sort, Concatenate

Implementation

```
    function Test_Aux is new Make_Test_Both(Test);
    function Merge_Aux is new Algorithms.Merge(Test_Aux);
begin
    return Merge_Aux(S1, S2);
end Merge;
```

6.5.44   MISMATCH

Specification

```
generic
with function Test(X, Y : Element) return Boolean;
procedure Mismatch(S1, S2: in Sequence;
                   S3, S4 : out Sequence);
```

Description   S1 and S2 are scanned in parallel until the first position is found at which they disagree, using Test as the test for element equality. S3 and S4 are set to be the subsequences of S1 and S2, respectively, beginning at this disagreement position and going to the end. S1 and S2 are shared.

Time   order $\min(n_1, n_2)m$

Space   0

where $n_1 = \text{length(S1)}$ and $n_2 = \text{length(S2)}$ and m is the average time for Test

Mutative?   No

Shares?   Yes

Details   S3 and S4 are both set to Nil if S1 and S2 agree entirely.

See also   Equal

Examples

```
declare
    Temp_1, Temp_2 : Sequence;
    procedure Mismatch_Equal is new Mismatch(Test => "=");
begin
    Mismatch_Equal(Iota(10), Iota(10), Temp_1, Temp_2);
    Show_List(Temp_1); Show_List(Temp_2);
--
--

    Mismatch_Equal(Iota(10), Iota(11), Temp_1, Temp_2);
    Show_List(Temp_1); Show_List(Temp_2);
--
--    10
    Mismatch_Equal(Invert(Iota(10)),
        Iota(10), Temp_1, Temp_2);
    Show_List(Temp_1); Show_List(Temp_2);
--    9 8 7 6 5 4 3 2 1 0
```

```
--  0  1  2  3  4  5  6  7  8  9
    Mismatch_Equal(Iota(10),Nil, Temp_1, Temp_2);
    Show_List(Temp_1); Show_List(Temp_2);
--  0  1  2  3  4  5  6  7  8  9
--
    Mismatch_Equal(Nil,Iota(10), Temp_1, Temp_2);
    Show_List(Temp_1); Show_List(Temp_2);
--
--  0  1  2  3  4  5  6  7  8  9
    Mismatch_Equal(Nil,Nil, Temp_1, Temp_2);
    Show_List(Temp_1); Show_List(Temp_2);
--
--
  end;
```

Implementation

```
    function Test_Aux is new Make_Test_Both(Test);
    procedure Mismatch_Aux is
        new Algorithms.Mismatch(Test_Aux);
begin
  Mismatch_Aux(S1, S2, S3, S4);
end Mismatch;
```

6.5.45   NEXT

Specification

```
function Next(S : Sequence)
      return Sequence renames Next0;
```

Description   Returns the sequence consisting of all the elements of S, except the first. S is shared.

Time   constant

Space   0

Mutative?   No

Shares?   Yes

Details   This description is actually a requirement on Next0, a generic formal parameter of the package. Raises an exception, Next_Of_Nil, if S is Nil.

See also   Set_Next, First

6.5.46 NOT_ANY

Specification

```
generic
with function Test(X : Element) return Boolean;
function Not_Any(S : Sequence)
        return Boolean;
```

Description   Returns true if Test is false of every element of S, false otherwise. Elements numbered 0, 1, 2, ... are tried in order.

Time   order nm

Space   0

   where $n = \text{length}(S)$and m is the average time for Test

Mutative?   No

Shares?   No

Details   Returns true if S is Nil.

See also   Every, Some, Not_Every

Examples

```
declare
    function Not_Any_Odd is new Not_Any(Test => Odd);
    function Delete_If_Odd is new Delete_If(Test => Odd);
  begin
    Show_Boolean(Not_Any_Odd(Iota(10)));
--False
    Show_Boolean(Not_Any_Odd(Delete_If_Odd(Iota(10))));
--True
  end;
```

Implementation

```
   function Test_Aux is new Make_Test_If(Test);
   function Not_Any_Aux is new Algorithms.Not_Any(Test_Aux);
begin
  return Not_Any_Aux(S);
end Not_Any;
```

6.5.47 NOT_EVERY

Specification

```
generic
with function Test(X : Element) return Boolean;
function Not_Every(S : Sequence)
        return Boolean;
```

Description   Returns true if Test is false of some element of S, false otherwise. Elements numbered 0, 1, 2, ... are tried in order.

Time   order nm

Space   0

>   **where** $n = $ length(S)and m is the average time for Test

Mutative?   No

Shares?   No

Details   Returns false if S is Nil.

See also   Every, Some

Examples

```
declare
    function Not_Every_Odd is new Not_Every(Test => Odd);
    function Delete_If_Not_Odd is
        new Delete_If_Not(Test => Odd);
begin
  Show_Boolean(Not_Every_Odd(Iota(10)));
--True
  Show_Boolean(
      Not_Every_Odd(Delete_If_Not_Odd(Iota(10))));
--False
 end;
```

Implementation

```
  function Test_Aux is new Make_Test_If(Test);
  function Not_Every_Aux is
      new Algorithms.Not_Every(Test_Aux);
begin
 return Not_Every_Aux(S);
end Not_Every;
```

6.5.48 NTH

Specification

```
function Nth(N : Integer; S : Sequence)
      return Element;
```

Description   Returns the N-th element of S.

Time   order N

Space   0

Mutative?   No

Shares?   No

Details   The numbering of elements begins with 0, hence Nth(0,S) is the same as First(S) and Nth(Length(S)-1,S) is the same as First(Last(S)). An exception, Next_Of_Nil, is raised if N > Length(S) − 1. If N < 0, First(S) is returned.

See also   Nth_Rest

Implementation

```
begin
  return First(Nth_Rest(N, S));
end Nth;
```

6.5.49 NTH_REST

Specification

```
function Nth_Rest(N : Integer; S : Sequence)
       return Sequence;
```

Description   Returns a sequence containing the elements of S numbered
N, N+1, ..., Length(S)-1.

Time   order N

Space   order N

Mutative?   No

Shares?   Yes

Details   The numbering of elements begins with 0, hence Nth_Rest(0,S)
is the same as S and Nth_Rest(Length(S)-1,S) is the same as Last(S).
An exception, Next_Of_Nil, is raised if N > Length(S) − 1. If N < 0, S is
returned.

See also   Nth, Butlast, Butlast_Copy

Implementation

```
begin
  return Algorithms.Nth_Rest(N, S);
end Nth_Rest;
```

6.5.50   POSITION

Specification

```
generic
with function Test(X, Y : Element) return Boolean;
function Position(Item : Element; S : Sequence)
        return Integer;
```

Description   If S contains an element E such that Test(Item,E) is true, then the index of the leftmost such item is returned; otherwise -1 is returned.

Time   order nm

Space   0

> **where** $n = $ length(S)and m is the average time for Test

Mutative?   No

Shares?   No

Details   The index of the first item is 0, of the last is length(S)-1.

See also   Position_If, Position_If_Not, Find, Some, Search

Examples

```
declare
  function Position_When_Greater is
      new Position(Test => "<");
begin

  Show_Integer(Position_When_Greater(3, Iota(7)));
--   4
end;
```

Implementation

```
  function Test_Aux is new Make_Test(Item, Test);
  function Position_Aux is
      new Algorithms.Position(Test_Aux);
begin
  return Position_Aux(S);
end Position;
```

6.5.51 POSITION_IF

Specification

```
generic
with function Test(X : Element) return Boolean;
function Position_If(S : Sequence)
        return Integer;
```

Description   If S contains an element E such that Test(E) is true, then the index of the leftmost such item is returned; otherwise -1 is returned.

Time   order nm

Space   0

> where $n = \text{length}(S)$and m is the average time for Test

Mutative?   No

Shares?   No

Details   The index of the first item is 0, of the last is length(S)-1.

See also   Position_If_Not, Position, Find, Some, Search

Examples

```
declare
    function Position_If_Greater_Than_7 is
        new Position_If(Test => Greater_Than_7);
begin
  Show_Integer(Position_If_Greater_Than_7(Iota(10)));
--  8
end;
```

Implementation

```
  function Test_Aux is new Make_Test_If(Test);
  function Position_Aux is
      new Algorithms.Position(Test_Aux);
begin
  return Position_Aux(S);
end Position_If;
```

6.5.52   POSITION_IF_NOT

Specification

```
generic
with function Test(X : Element) return Boolean;
function Position_If_Not(S : Sequence)
        return Integer;
```

Description   If S contains an element E such that Test(E) is false, then the index of the leftmost such item is returned; otherwise -1 is returned.

Time   order nm

Space   0

   where $n = $ length(S)and m is the average time for Test

Mutative?   No

Shares?   No

Details   The index of the first item is 0, of the last is length(S)-1.

See also   Position_If_Not, Position, Find, Some, Search

Examples

```
declare
    function Position_If_Not_Greater_Than_7 is
        new Position_If_Not(Test=>Greater_Than_7);
begin
  Show_Integer(
      Position_If_Not_Greater_Than_7(Invert(Iota(10))));
--   2
end;
```

Implementation

```
  function Test_Aux is new Make_Test_If_Not(Test);
  function Position_Aux is
      new Algorithms.Position(Test_Aux);
begin
  return Position_Aux(S);
end Position_If_Not;
```

6.5.53 REDUCE

Specification

```
generic
Identity : Element;
with function F(X, Y : Element) return Element;
function Reduce(S : Sequence)
        return Element;
```

Description   Combines all the elements of S using F; for example, using
"+" for F and 0 for Identity one can add up a sequence of Integers.

Time   order nm

Space   0

    where $n = $ length(S)and m is the average time for Test

Mutative?   No

Shares?   No

See also   For_Each, Map

Examples

```
declare
  function Reduce_Times is
      new Reduce(Identity => 1, F => "*");
  function Reduce_Plus is
      new Reduce(Identity => 0, F => "+");
begin
  Show_Integer(Reduce_Times(Next(Iota(5))));
--   24
  Show_Integer(Reduce_Plus(Iota(100)));
--   4950
end;
```

Implementation

```
function F_Aux(X : Element; S : Sequence)
    return Element is
begin
  return F(X, First(S));
end F_Aux;
pragma Inline(F_Aux);
function Reduce_Aux
  is new Algorithms.Accumulate(Element, F_Aux);
begin
if Is_End(S) then
  return Identity;
end if;
return Reduce_Aux(Next(S), First(S));
end Reduce;
```

6.5.54 REVERSE_APPEND

Specification

```
function Reverse_Append(S1, S2 : Sequence)
       return Sequence;
```

Description   Returns a sequence consisting of the elements of S1, in reverse order, followed by those of S2 in order. S2 is shared.

Time   order n_1

Space   order n_1

where $n_1 = \text{length}(S1)$

Mutative?   No

Shares?   Yes

See also   Reverse_Concatenate

Implementation

```
begin
  return Algorithms.Reverse_Append(S1, S2);
end Reverse_Append;
```

6.5.55 REVERSE_CONCATENATE

Specification

```
function Reverse_Concatenate(S1, S2 : Sequence)
      return Sequence;
```

Description   Returns a sequence consisting of the elements of S1, in reverse order, followed by those of S2 in order. S1 is mutated and S2 is shared.

Time   order n_1

Space   0

    where $n_1 = \text{length(S1)}$

Mutative?   Yes

Shares?   Yes

See also   Reverse_Append

Examples

```
    Show_List(Reverse_Concatenate(Iota(5), Iota(6)));
--  4  3  2  1  0  0  1  2  3  4  5
    Show_List(Reverse_Concatenate(Nil, Iota(6)));
--  0  1  2  3  4  5
    Show_List(Reverse_Concatenate(Iota(5), Nil));
--  4  3  2  1  0
```

Implementation

```
begin
  return Algorithms.Reverse_Concatenate(S1, S2);
end Reverse_Concatenate;
```

6.5.56   SEARCH

Specification

```
generic
with function Test(X, Y : Element) return Boolean;
function Search(S1, S2 : Sequence)
        return Sequence;
```

Description   Returns the leftmost occurrence of a subsequence in S2
that element-wise matches S1, using Test as the the test for element-
wise equality. If no matching subsequence is found, Nil is returned.

Time   order nm

Space   0

   where $n = $ length(S)and m is the average time for Test

Mutative?   No

Shares?   Yes

See also   Position, Find, Some, Search

Examples

```
declare
    function Search_Equal is new Search(Test => "=");
  begin
    Show_List(Search_Equal(Construct(7,
        Construct(8, Construct(9, Nil))), Iota(12)));
--   7  8  9  10  11
  end;
```

Implementation

```
    function Test_Aux is new Make_Test_Both(Test);
    function Search_Aux is new Algorithms.Search(Test_Aux);
  begin
    return Search_Aux(S1, S2);
  end Search;
```

6.5.57   SET_FIRST

Specification

```
procedure Set_First(S : Sequence; E : Element)
    renames Set_First0;
```

Description   Changes S so that its first element is E but the following elements are unchanged.

Time   constant

Space   0

Mutative?   Yes

Shares?   No

Details   This description is actually a requirement on Set_Next0, which is a generic formal parameter of the package. Raises an exception, Set_First_Of_Nil, if S is Nil.

See also   Next, Set_First

6.5.58 SET_NEXT

Specification

```
procedure Set_Next(S1, S2 : Sequence) renames Set_Next0;
```

Description   Changes S1 so that its first element is unchanged but the
following elements are those of S2. S2 is shared.

Time   constant

Space   0

Mutative?   Yes

Shares?   Yes

Details   This description is actually a requirement on Set_Next0, which is
a generic formal parameter of the package. Raises an exception, Set_Next_Of_Nil,
if S1 is Nil.

See also   Next, Set_First

6.5.59   SET_NTH

Specification

```
procedure Set_Nth(S: Sequence;
    Index: Integer; New_Item: Element);
```

Description   Replaces the element of S specified by Index with New_-
Item. S is mutated.

Time   order Index

Space   0

Mutative?   Yes

Shares?   No

Details   The numbering of elements begins with 0, hence Set_Nth(0,S,X)
is the same as Set_First(S,X) and Set_Nth(Length(S)-1,S,X) is the same
as Set_First(Last(S),X). An exception, Next_Of_Nil, is raised if S has
fewer than Index+1 elements.

See also   Nth

Implementation

```
begin
  Set_First(Nth_Rest(Index, S), New_Item);
end Set_Nth;
```

6.5.60 SOME

Specification

```
generic
with function Test(X : Element) return Boolean;
function Some(S : Sequence)
        return Boolean;
```

Description   Returns true if Test is true of some element of S, false otherwise. Elements numbered 0, 1, 2, ... are tried in order.

Time   order nm

Space   0

> where $n = $ length(S)and m is the average time for Test

Mutative?   No

Shares?   No

Details   Returns false if S is Nil.

See also   Not_Every, Every, Not_Any

Examples

```
declare
   function Some_Odd is new Some(Test => Odd);
   function Delete_If_Odd is new Delete_If(Test => Odd);
 begin
   Show_Boolean(Some_Odd(Iota(10)));
--True
   Show_Boolean(Some_Odd(Delete_If_Odd(Iota(10))));
--False
 end;
```

Implementation

```
   function Test_Aux is new Make_Test_If(Test);
   function Some_Aux is new Algorithms.Some(Test_Aux);
 begin
   return Some_Aux(S);
 end Some;
```

6.5.61   SORT

Specification

```
generic
with function Test(X, Y : Element) return Boolean;
function Sort(S : Sequence)
        return Sequence;
```

Description   Returns a sequence containing the same elements as S, but in order as determined by Test. S is mutated.

Time   order $(n \log n)m$

Space   0

   where $n =$ length(S)and m is the average time for Test

Mutative?   Yes

Shares?   No

Details   This is a stable sort. See Section 6.1.7 for discussion of the restrictions on Test and definition of "in order as determined by Test."

See also   Merge

Examples

```
declare
    function Sort_Ascending is new Sort(Test => "<");
    function Shuffle_Merge is
        new Merge(Test => Shuffle_Test);
  begin
    Show_List(Sort_Ascending(
        Shuffle_Merge(Iota(5), Invert(Iota(5)))));
-- 0  0  1  1  2  2  3  3  4  4
  end;
```

Implementation

```
  function Test_Aux is new Make_Test_Both(Test);
  function Sort_Aux is
      new Algorithms.Sort(32, Nil, Test_Aux);
begin
  return Sort_Aux(S);
end Sort;
```

6.5.62 SUBSEQUENCE

Specification

```
function Subsequence(S : Sequence; Start, Stop : Integer)
       return Sequence;
```

Description   Returns a sequence consisting of the elements of S numbered Start through Stop-1.

Time   order Stop

Space   order Stop - Start

Mutative?   No

Shares?   No

Details   Start and Stop should satisfy $0 \leq$ Start $\leq$ Stop $\leq$ Length(S). The numbering of elements begins with 0, hence Subsequence(S, 0, Length(S)) is a copy of S. An exception, Next_Of_Nil, is raised if Stop $>$ Length(S).

See also   Butlast, Butlast_Copy, Copy_First_N

Examples

```
    Show_List(Subsequence(Iota(10), 2, 5));
--  2  3  4
```

Implementation

```
begin
  return Copy_First_N(Nth_Rest(Start, S), Stop - Start);
end Subsequence;
```

6.5.63 SUBSTITUTE

Specification

```
generic
with function Test(X, Y : Element) return Boolean;
function Substitute(New_Item, Old_Item: Element;
    S: Sequence) return Sequence;
```

Description   Returns a sequence of the elements of S except that those
E such that Test(Old_Item,E) is true are replaced by New_Item. S is
mutated.

Time   order nm

Space   0

where $n = $ length(S)and m is the average time for Test

Mutative?   Yes

Shares?   No

See also   Substitute_Copy, Substitute_If, Substitute_If_Not

Examples

```
declare
    function Substitute_When_Divides
              is new Substitute(Test => Divides);
  begin
    Show_List(Substitute_When_Divides(-1, 3, Iota(15)));
--  -1  1  2 -1  4  5 -1  7  8 -1  10  11 -1  13  14
  end;
```

Implementation

```
    procedure The_Procedure_Aux(S : Sequence) is
    begin
      if Test(Old_Item, First(S)) then
        Set_First(S, New_Item);
      end if;
    end The_Procedure_Aux;
    pragma Inline(The_Procedure_Aux);
    procedure Nsub_Aux
      is new Algorithms.For_Each_Cell(The_Procedure_Aux);
  begin
    Nsub_Aux(S);
    return (S);
  end Substitute;
```

6.5.64   SUBSTITUTE_COPY

Specification

```
generic
with function Test(X, Y : Element) return Boolean;
function Substitute_Copy(New_Item, Old_Item: Element;
    S: Sequence) return Sequence;
```

Description   Returns a sequence of the elements of S except that those E such that Test(Old_Item,E) is true are replaced by New_Item.

Time   order nm

Space   order n

   where $n = $ length(S)and m is the average time for Test

Mutative?   No

Shares?   No

See also   Substitute, Substitute_Copy_If, Substitute_Copy_If_Not

Examples

```
declare
   function Substitute_Copy_When_Divides
            is new Substitute_Copy(Test => Divides);
 begin
   Show_List(
      Substitute_Copy_When_Divides(-1, 3, Iota(15)));
-- -1  1  2 -1  4  5 -1  7  8 -1  10  11 -1  13  14
 end;
```

Implementation

```
   function F_Aux(X : Element) return Element is
   begin
     if Test(Old_Item, X) then
       return New_Item;
     else
       return X;
     end if;
   end F_Aux;
   pragma Inline(F_Aux);
   function Subst_Aux is new Map_Copy(F_Aux);
 begin
   return Subst_Aux(S);
 end Substitute_Copy;
```

6.5.65   SUBSTITUTE_COPY_IF

Specification

```
generic
with function Test(X : Element) return Boolean;
function Substitute_Copy_If(New_Item: Element; S: Sequence)
    return Sequence;
```

Description   Returns a sequence of the elements of S except that those E such that Test(E) is true are replaced by New_Item.

Time   order nm

Space   order n

> **where** $n = $ length(S)and m is the average time for Test

Mutative?   No

Shares?   No

See also   Substitute_Copy_If_Not, Substitute_If, Substitute_Copy

Examples

```
declare
    function Substitute_Copy_If_Odd
              is new Substitute_Copy_If(Test => Odd);
  begin
    Show_List(Substitute_Copy_If_Odd(-1, Iota(15)));
--   0 -1  2 -1  4 -1  6 -1  8 -1  10 -1  12 -1  14
  end;
```

Implementation

```
    function F_Aux(X : Element) return Element is
    begin
      if Test(X) then
        return New_Item;
      else
        return X;
      end if;
    end F_Aux;
    pragma Inline(F_Aux);
    function Subst_Aux is new Map_Copy(F_Aux);
  begin
    return Subst_Aux(S);
  end Substitute_Copy_If;
```

6.5.66   SUBSTITUTE_COPY_IF_NOT

Specification

```
generic
with function Test(X : Element) return Boolean;
function Substitute_Copy_If_Not(New_Item: Element;
    S: Sequence) return Sequence;
```

Description   Returns a sequence of the elements of S except that those E such that Test(E) is false are replaced by New_Item.

Time   order nm

Space   order n

where $n =$ length(S)and m is the average time for Test

Mutative?   No

Shares?   No

See also   Substitute_Copy_If, Substitute_If_Not, Substitute_Copy

Examples

```
declare
    function Substitute_Copy_If_Not_Odd
            is new Substitute_Copy_If_Not(Test => Odd);
  begin
    Show_List(Substitute_Copy_If_Not_Odd(-1, Iota(15)));
--   -1   1 -1   3 -1   5 -1   7 -1   9 -1   11 -1   13 -1
  end;
```

Implementation

```
    function F_Aux(X : Element) return Element is
    begin
      if Test(X) then
        return X;
      else
        return New_Item;
      end if;
    end F_Aux;
    pragma Inline(F_Aux);
    function Subst_Aux is new Map_Copy(F_Aux);
  begin
    return Subst_Aux(S);
  end Substitute_Copy_If_Not;
```

6.5.67   SUBSTITUTE_IF

Specification

```
generic
with function Test(X : Element) return Boolean;
function Substitute_If(New_Item : Element; S : Sequence)
        return Sequence;
```

Description   Returns a sequence of the elements of S except that those E such that Test(E) is true are replaced by New_Item. S is mutated.

Time   order nm

Space   0

where $n = $ length(S)and m is the average time for Test

Mutative?   Yes

Shares?   No

See also   Substitute_If_Not, Substitute, Substitute_Copy

Examples

```
declare
    function Substitute_If_Odd is new Substitute_If(Test => Odd);
  begin
    Show_List(Substitute_If_Odd(-1, Iota(15)));
--  0 -1  2 -1  4 -1  6 -1  8 -1  10 -1  12 -1  14
  end;
```

Implementation

```
    procedure The_Procedure_Aux(S : Sequence) is
    begin
      if Test(First(S)) then
        Set_First(S, New_Item);
      end if;
    end The_Procedure_Aux;
    pragma Inline(The_Procedure_Aux);
    procedure Nsub_Aux
      is new Algorithms.For_Each_Cell(The_Procedure_Aux);
  begin
    Nsub_Aux(S);
    return S;
  end Substitute_If;
```

6.5.68   SUBSTITUTE_IF_NOT

Specification

```
generic
with function Test(X : Element) return Boolean;
function Substitute_If_Not(New_Item: Element; S: Sequence)
      return Sequence;
```

Description   Returns a sequence of the elements of S except that those E such that Test(E) is false are replaced by New_Item. S is mutated.

Time   order nm

Space   0

>   where $n = \text{length}(S)$ and m is the average time for Test

Mutative?   Yes

Shares?   No

See also   Substitute_If, Substitute, Substitute_Copy

Examples

```
declare
   function Substitute_If_Not_Odd
            is new Substitute_If_Not(Test => Odd);
 begin
   Show_List(Substitute_If_Not_Odd(-1, Iota(15)));
-- -1  1 -1  3 -1  5 -1  7 -1  9 -1  11 -1  13 -1
 end;
```

Implementation

```
   procedure The_Procedure_Aux(S : Sequence) is
   begin
     if not Test(First(S)) then
       Set_First(S, New_Item);
     end if;
   end The_Procedure_Aux;
   pragma Inline(The_Procedure_Aux);
   procedure Nsub_Aux
     is new Algorithms.For_Each_Cell(The_Procedure_Aux);
 begin
   Nsub_Aux(S);
   return S;
 end Substitute_If_Not;
```

7

Linked List Algorithms Package

7.1 Overview

This is a generic algorithms package that provides 31 algorithms for manipulating a linked list representation of sequences. Only a singly-linked representation is assumed, but many of the algorithms can also reasonably be used with other representations such as circular or non-circular doubly-linked representations. As can be seen from the subprogram implementations in the previous chapter, even for a singly-linked representation these algorithms can be instantiated in various ways to produce a substantially larger collection of useful operations.

Generic algorithm packages such as this are mainly for use in building the library, but nonetheless we include their full descriptions since they illustrate many principles of component reuse in addition to allowing the programmer to be fully aware of the algorithms used. Programmers familiar with the details of these algorithms and the principles of the library structure may also want to consider direct use of generic algorithms packages in some situations.

Perhaps the most interesting aspect of this package is the fact that more than 30 useful algorithms have been programmed entirely in terms of only four primitive operations, which have been made generic formal parameters along with a type, `Cell`:

- `function Next(S : Cell) return Cell;`

- `procedure Set_Next(S1, S2 : Cell);`

- `function Is_End(S : Cell) return Boolean;`

- `function Copy_Cell(S1, S2 : Cell) return Cell;`

It is assumed that

- `Next(S)` returns the sequence of cells of `S` except for its first cell;

- `Set_Next(S1, S2)` changes `S1` so that it retains its first cell but the following cells are all of those of `S2`;

- `Is_End(S)` returns true if `S` is the empty sequence of cells; false otherwise; and

- Copy_Cell(S1, S2) returns a sequence starting with a new cell containing some information from the first cell of S1; the following cells are those of S2.

All of the manipulation of *data* is therefore isolated in Copy_Cell.

Most of the algorithms in this package are straightforward; nevertheless, there is a major advantage of having them in a library since there are many small details that must be programmed correctly. Two of the operations, Merge_Non_Empty, and Sort, are of substantial interest from an algorithmic point of view. The Sort operation uses a merge-sort algorithm. In merge-sorting, it is essential that merging is always performed on sequences of the same length whenever possible, in order to produce $n \log n$ time behavior. With linked-lists this could be accomplished by traversing the initial list in order to divide it in two, and so on recursively, but this approach is both clumsy and inefficient (neither of which has prevented it from appearing in some textbooks). Instead, we employ a "binary counter" technique: an array, Register, is kept in which Register(I) always holds either an empty sequence or one of length 2^I, and single element sequences are "added" to the "count" in the register, with carries taking the form of merging of equal-length sequences.

7.2   Package specification

The package specification is as follows:

```
generic

   type Cell is private;
   with function Next(S : Cell) return Cell;
   with procedure Set_Next(S1, S2 : Cell);
   with function Is_End(S : Cell) return Boolean;
   with function Copy_Cell(S1, S2 : Cell) return Cell;

package Linked_List_Algorithms is


 {The subprogram specifications}

end Linked_List_Algorithms;
```

7.3   Package body

The package body is as follows:

```
package body Linked_List_Algorithms is

 {The subprogram bodies}

end Linked_List_Algorithms;
```

7.4   Subprograms

7.4.1   ACCUMULATE

Specification

```
generic
     type Element is private;
  with function F(X : Element; Y : Cell) return Element;
function Accumulate(S : Cell; Initial_Value : Element)
     return Element;
```

Description   Puts Initial_Value into an accumulator and successively updates the accumulator with F(accumulator,X) for each cell X of S.

Time   order nm

Space   0

> **where** $n = \text{length(S)}$ and f is the average time for F

Mutative?   No

Shares?   No

See also   For_Each_Cell, Map

Implementation

```
   To_Be_Done : Cell     := S;
   Result     : Element := Initial_Value;
begin
  while not Is_End(To_Be_Done) loop
    Result := F(Result, To_Be_Done);
    Advance(To_Be_Done);
  end loop;
  return Result;
end Accumulate;
```

7.4.2   ADVANCE

Specification

```
procedure Advance(S : in out Cell);
pragma inline(Advance);
```

Description   Changes S to Next(S).

Time   constant

Space   0

Mutative?   No

Shares?   Yes

Details   Used for traversing a sequence, nondestructively—does not free any cells.

See also   Next

Implementation

```
begin
  S := Next(S);
end Advance;
```

7.4.3 APPEND

Specification

```
function Append(S1, S2 : Cell)
       return Cell;
```

Description   Returns a sequence containing copies of all the cells of S1 followed by the cells of S2. S2 is shared.

Time   order n_1

Space   order n_1

   where $n_1 = \text{length}(S1)$

Mutative?   No

Shares?   Yes

See also   Append_First_N, Reverse_Append

Implementation

```
   Result, Current : Cell;
   To_Be_Done      : Cell := S1;
 begin
   if Is_End(S1) then
     return S2;
   end if;
   Result := Copy_Cell(To_Be_Done, S2);
   Current := Result;
   loop
     Advance(To_Be_Done);
     if Is_End(To_Be_Done) then
       return Result;
     end if;
     Attach_To_Tail(Current, Copy_Cell(To_Be_Done, S2));
   end loop;
 end Append;
```

7.4.4   APPEND_FIRST_N

Specification

```
function Append_First_N(S1, S2 : Cell; N : Integer)
        return Cell;
```

Description   Returns a sequence containing the first N cells of S1 followed by all the cells of S2. S2 is shared.

Time   order n_1

Space   order n_1

   where $n_1 = \min(\text{N}, \text{length}(\text{S1}))$

Mutative?   No

Shares?   Yes

See also   Append

Implementation

```
    Result, Current, Temp : Cell;
    To_Be_Done            : Cell    := S1;
    I                     : Integer := N - 1;
  begin
    if Is_End(S1) or else I < 0 then
      return S2;
    end if;
    Result := Copy_Cell(To_Be_Done, S2);
    Current := Result;
    loop
      Advance(To_Be_Done);
      I := I - 1;
      if Is_End(To_Be_Done) or else I < 0 then
        return Result;
      end if;
      Attach_To_Tail(Current, Copy_Cell(To_Be_Done, S2));
    end loop;
  end Append_First_N;
```

7.4.5   ATTACH_TO_TAIL

Specification

```
procedure Attach_To_Tail(X : in out Cell; Y : in Cell);
pragma inline(Attach_To_Tail);
```

Description   Performs Set_Next(X,Y) followed by X := Y.

Time   constant

Space   0

Mutative?   Yes

Shares?   Yes

See also

Implementation

```
begin
  Set_Next(X, Y);
  X := Y;
end Attach_To_Tail;
```

7.4.6 COUNT

Specification

```
generic
      with function Test(X : Cell) return Boolean;
function Count(S : Cell)
        return Integer;
```

Description   Returns a non-negative integer equal to the number of cells X of S such that Test(X) is true.

Time   order nm

Space   0

> **where** $n = \text{length(S)}$ and m is the average time for Test

Mutative?   No

Shares?   No

See also   Find

Implementation

```
    Result     : Integer := 0;
    To_Be_Done : Cell     := S;
  begin
    while not Is_End(To_Be_Done) loop
      if Test(To_Be_Done) then
        Result := Result + 1;
      end if;
      Advance(To_Be_Done);
    end loop;
    return Result;
  end Count;
```

7.4.7 DELETE_COPY_APPEND

Specification

```
generic
     with function Test(X : Cell) return Boolean;
function Delete_Copy_Append(S1, S2 : Cell)
        return Cell;
```

Description   Returns a sequence consisting of copies of all the cells X of S1 except those for which Test(X) is true, followed by all the cells of S2. S2 is shared.

Time   order nm

Space   order n

   where $n = $ length(S)and m is the average time for Test

Mutative?   No

Shares?   Yes

See also   Delete, Append

Implementation

```
   To_Be_Done       : Cell := S1;
   Result, Current : Cell;
begin
  while not Is_End(To_Be_Done)
      and then Test(To_Be_Done) loop
    Advance(To_Be_Done);
  end loop;
  if Is_End(To_Be_Done) then
    return To_Be_Done;
  end if;
  Result := Copy_Cell(To_Be_Done, S2);
  Current := Result;
  Advance(To_Be_Done);
  while not Is_End(To_Be_Done) loop
    if not Test(To_Be_Done) then
      Attach_To_Tail(Current, Copy_Cell(To_Be_Done, S2));
    end if;
    Advance(To_Be_Done);
  end loop;
  return Result;
end Delete_Copy_Append;
```

7.4.8   DELETE_COPY_DUPLICATES_APPEND

Specification

```
generic
     with function Test(X, Y : Cell) return Boolean;
function Delete_Copy_Duplicates_Append(S1, S2 : Cell)
     return Cell;
```

Description   Returns a sequence of copies of the cells of S1 but with only one occurrence of each, using Test as the test for equality, followed by all the cells of S2. S2 is shared.

Time   order $n^2 m$

Space   order n

where $n = \text{length(S)}$ and m is the average time for Test

Mutative?   No

Shares?   Yes

Details   The left-most occurrence of each duplicated item is retained. Copy_Cell (a generic parameter of the package) is used to do the copying.

See also   Delete_Duplicates

Implementation

```
   Result, Current, I : Cell;
   To_Be_Done          : Cell := S1;
begin
  if Is_End(S1) then
    return S1;
  end if;
  Result := Copy_Cell(To_Be_Done, S2);
  Current := Result;
  Advance(To_Be_Done);
  while not Is_End(To_Be_Done) loop
    I := Result;
    while not Is_End(I)
        and then not Test(I, To_Be_Done) loop
      Advance(I);
    end loop;
    if Is_End(I) then
      Attach_To_Tail(Current, Copy_Cell(To_Be_Done, S2));
    end if;
    Advance(To_Be_Done);
  end loop;
  return Result;
end Delete_Copy_Duplicates_Append;
```

7.4.9   DELETE_DUPLICATES

Specification

```
generic
     with function Test(X, Y : Cell) return Boolean;
  with procedure Free(X : Cell);
function Delete_Duplicates(S : Cell)
        return Cell;
```

Description   Returns a sequence of the cells of S but with only one occurrence of each, using Test as the test for equality. S is mutated.

Time   order n^2m

Space   0

    where $n = \text{length(S)}$ and m is the average time for Test

Mutative?   Yes

Shares?   No

Details   The left-most occurrence of each duplicated cell is retained.

See also   Delete_Copy_Duplicates

Implementation

```
   Tail, To_Be_Done, I : Cell := S;
 begin
   if not Is_End(To_Be_Done) then
     Advance(To_Be_Done);
     while not Is_End(To_Be_Done) loop
       I := S;
       while I /= To_Be_Done
           and then not Test(I, To_Be_Done) loop
         Advance(I);
       end loop;
       if I = To_Be_Done then
         Tail := To_Be_Done;
         Advance(To_Be_Done);
       else
         I := To_Be_Done;
         Advance(To_Be_Done);
         Set_Next(Tail, To_Be_Done);
         Free(I);
       end if;
     end loop;
   end if;
   return S;
 end Delete_Duplicates;
```

7.4.10   EQUAL

Specification

```
generic
     with function Test(X, Y : Cell) return Boolean;
function Equal(S1, S2 : Cell)
       return Boolean;
```

Description   Returns true if S1 and S2 are of the same length and for each position the cells in that position in S1 and S2 are equal, using Test as the test for cell equality.

Time   order $m \min(\mathrm{length}(S1), \mathrm{length}(S2))$

Space   0

    where m is the average time for Test

Mutative?   No

Shares?   No

See also   Mismatch

Implementation

```
   Tail_1, Tail_2 : Cell;
   procedure Mismatch_Aux is new Mismatch(Test);
begin
   Mismatch_Aux(S1, S2, Tail_1, Tail_2);
   return Is_End(Tail_1) and Is_End(Tail_2);
end Equal;
```

7.4.11   EVERY

Specification

```
generic
     with function Test(X : Cell) return Boolean;
function Every(S : Cell)
     return Boolean;
```

Description   Returns true if Test is true of every cell of S, false otherwise. Cells numbered 0, 1, 2, ... are tried in order.

Time   order nm

Space   0

> **where** $n = \text{length}(S)$ and m is the average time for Test

Mutative?   No

Shares?   No

Details   Returns true if Is_End(S) is true.

See also   Not_Every, Some

Implementation

```
   To_Be_Done : Cell := S;
begin
   while not Is_End(To_Be_Done)
       and then Test(To_Be_Done) loop
     Advance(To_Be_Done);
   end loop;
   return Is_End(To_Be_Done);
end Every;
```

7.4.12   FIND

Specification

```
generic
      with function Test(X : Cell) return Boolean;
function Find(S : Cell)
         return Cell;
```

Description   If S contains an cell X such that Test(X) is true, then the sequence of cells of S beginning with the leftmost such cell is returned; otherwise a cell X such that Is_End(X) is true is returned.

Time   order nm

Space   0

where $n = $ length(S)and m is the average time for Test

Mutative?   No

Shares?   Yes

See also   Some, Search

Implementation

```
   To_Be_Done : Cell := S;
 begin
   while not Is_End(To_Be_Done)
       and then not Test(To_Be_Done) loop
     Advance(To_Be_Done);
   end loop;
   return To_Be_Done;
 end Find;
```

7.4.13   FOR_EACH_CELL

Specification

```
generic
      with procedure The_Procedure(X : Cell);
procedure For_Each_Cell(S : Cell);
```

Description   Applies The_Procedure to each cell of S.

Time   order np

Space   0

where $n = $ length(S) and p is the average time for The_Procedure

Mutative?   No

Shares?   No

Details   0

See also   For_Each_Cell_2, Map

Implementation

```
   To_Be_Done : Cell := S;
   Temp       : Cell;
begin
  while not Is_End(To_Be_Done) loop
    Temp := Next(To_Be_Done);
    The_Procedure(To_Be_Done);
    To_Be_Done := Temp;
  end loop;
end For_Each_Cell;
```

7.4.14   FOR_EACH_CELL_2

Specification

```
generic
      with procedure The_Procedure(X, Y : Cell);
procedure For_Each_Cell_2(S1, S2 : Cell);
```

Description   Applies The_Procedure to pairs of cells of S1 and S2 in the same position.

Time   order np

Space   order n

where $n_1 = \text{length}(S1)$, $n_2 = \text{length}(S2)$, $n = \min(n_1, n_2)$, and p is the average time for The_Procedure

Mutative?   No

Shares?   No

Details   Stops when a cell X is reached in either of S1 or S2 such that Is_End(X) is true.

See also   For_Each_Cell, Map_2

Implementation

```
   To_Be_Done1 : Cell := S1;
   To_Be_Done2 : Cell := S2;
   Temp_1      : Cell;
   Temp_2      : Cell;
begin
  while not Is_End(To_Be_Done1)
        and then not Is_End(To_Be_Done2) loop
    Temp_1 := Next(To_Be_Done1);
    Temp_2 := Next(To_Be_Done2);
    The_Procedure(To_Be_Done1, To_Be_Done2);
    To_Be_Done1 := Temp_1;
    To_Be_Done2 := Temp_2;
  end loop;
end For_Each_Cell_2;
```

7.4.15   INVERT_PARTITION

Specification

```
generic
     with function Test(S: Cell) return Boolean;
procedure Invert_Partition(S1: in Cell;
    S2, S3: in out Cell);
```

Description   Partitions the cells of S1 into two sequences S2 and S3 with those in S2 satisfying Test and those in S3 failing Test. The cells in S2 and S3 are in reverse order of their occurrence in S1. S1 is mutated.

Time nm

Space   0

   where $n = $ length(S)and m is the average time for Test

Mutative?   Yes

Shares?   Yes

See also   Invert

Implementation

```
   To_Be_Done, Temp: Cell := S1;
begin
   while not Is_End(To_Be_Done) loop
     Advance(To_Be_Done);
     if Test(Temp) then
       Set_Next(Temp, S2);
       S2 := Temp;
     else
       Set_Next(Temp, S3);
       S3 := Temp;
     end if;
     Temp := To_Be_Done;
   end loop;
end Invert_Partition;
```

7.4.16   LAST

Specification

```
function Last(S : Cell)
       return Cell;
```

Description   Returns the sequence consisting of just the last cell of S.

Time   order n

Space   0

where $n = \text{length}(S)$

Mutative?   No

Shares?   Yes

Details   An attempt is made to compute Next(S) even if Is_End(S) is true.

See also

Implementation

```
   I, J : Cell := S;
 begin
   loop
     Advance(J);
     exit when Is_End(J);
     I := J;
   end loop;
   return I;
 end Last;
```

7.4.17   LENGTH

Specification

```
function Length(S : Cell)
       return Integer;
```

Description   The number of cells in S is returned as a non-negative integer.

Time   order n

Space   0

   where $n = \text{length}(S)$

Mutative?   No

Shares?   No

See also

Implementation

```
   Result     : Integer := 0;
   To_Be_Done : Cell    := S;
 begin
   while not Is_End(To_Be_Done) loop
     Result := Result + 1;
     Advance(To_Be_Done);
   end loop;
   return Result;
 end Length;
```

7.4.18   MAP_COPY_2_APPEND

Specification

```
generic
    with function Make_Cell(X, Y, Z : Cell) return Cell;
function Map_Copy_2_Append(S1, S2, S3 : Cell)
    return Cell;
```

Description   Returns a sequence of cells consisting of the results of applying Make_Cell cells of S1 followed by the cells of S2, using Make_Cell to do the copying. S2 is shared.

Time   order $n_1 + n_2$

Space   order n_1

 where $n_1 = \min(\text{length}(S1), \text{length}(S2))$ and $n_2 = \text{length}(S2)$

Mutative?   No

Shares?   Yes

Details   Each application of Make_Cell has a cell of S1 as its first argument, the corresponding cell of S2 as its second argument, and S3 as its third argument. Stops when a cell C in either S1 or S2 is reached such that Is_End(C) is true, ignoring any remaining cells in the other sequence.

See also   Append, Reverse_Append

Implementation

```
   Result, Current : Cell;
   To_Be_Done1      : Cell := S1;
   To_Be_Done2      : Cell := S2;
 begin
   if Is_End(To_Be_Done1) or else Is_End(To_Be_Done2) then
     return S3;
   end if;
   Result := Make_Cell(To_Be_Done1, To_Be_Done2, S3);
   Current := Result;
   Advance(To_Be_Done1);
   Advance(To_Be_Done2);
   while not Is_End(To_Be_Done1)
         and then not Is_End(To_Be_Done2) loop
     Attach_To_Tail(Current,
         Make_Cell(To_Be_Done1, To_Be_Done2, S3));
     Advance(To_Be_Done1);
     Advance(To_Be_Done2);
   end loop;
   return Result;
 end Map_Copy_2_Append;
```

7.4.19   MAP_COPY_APPEND

Specification

```
generic
     with function Make_Cell(X, Y : Cell) return Cell;
function Map_Copy_Append(S1, S2 : Cell)
        return Cell;
```

Description   Returns a sequence of cells consisting of the results of applying Make_Cell to the cells of S1 followed by the cells of S2.

Time   order $n_1 + n_2$

Space   order n_1

   where $n_1 = \text{length}(S1)$ and $n_2 = \text{length}(S2)$

Mutative?   No

Shares?   Yes

Details   Each application of Make_Cell has a cell of S1 as its first argument and S2 as its second argument.

See also   Append, Reverse_Append

Implementation

```
   Result, Current : Cell;
   To_Be_Done      : Cell := S1;
 begin
   if Is_End(To_Be_Done) then
     return S2;
   end if;
   Result := Make_Cell(To_Be_Done, S2);
   Current := Result;
   Advance(To_Be_Done);
   while not Is_End(To_Be_Done) loop
     Attach_To_Tail(Current, Make_Cell(To_Be_Done, S2));
     Advance(To_Be_Done);
   end loop;
   return Result;
 end Map_Copy_Append;
```

7.4.20 MERGE

Specification

```
generic
     with function Test(X, Y : Cell) return Boolean;
function Merge(S1, S2 : Cell)
        return Cell;
```

Description   Returns a sequence containing the same cells as S1 and S2, interleaved. If S1 and S2 are in order as determined by Test, the result is also. Both S1 and S2 are mutated.

Time   order $(n_1 + n_2)m$

Space   order $n_1 + n_2$

    where $n_1 = $ length(S1), $n_2 = $ length(S2), and m is the average time for Test

Mutative?   Yes

Shares?   No

Details   By "interleaved" is meant that if X precedes Y in S1 then X will precede Y in Merge(S1,S2) and similarly for X and Y in S2 (even if S1 or S2 is not in order). The property of stability also holds. See Section 6.1.7 for discussion of the restrictions on Test and definition of "in order as determined by Test."

See also   Merge_Non_Empty, Sort

Implementation

```
   function Merge_Aux is new Merge_Non_Empty(Test);
begin
  if Is_End(S1) then
    return S2;
  elsif Is_End(S2) then
    return S1;
  else
    return Merge_Aux(S1, S2);
  end if;
end Merge;
```

7.4.21   MERGE_NON_EMPTY

Specification

```
generic
     with function Test(X, Y : Cell) return Boolean;
function Merge_Non_Empty(S1, S2 : Cell)
        return Cell;
```

Description   Returns a sequence containing the same cells as S1 and S2, interleaved. If S1 and S2 are in order as determined by Test, the result is also. Both S1 and S2 are mutated.

Time   order $(n_1 + n_2)m$

Space   order $n_1 + n_2$

> **where** $n_1 = \text{length}(S1)$, $n_2 = \text{length}(S2)$, and m is the average time for Test

Mutative?   Yes

Shares?   No

Details   An attempt is made to compute Next(S1) even if Is_End(S1), and similarly for S2. (Merge avoids this potential problem; this subprogram exists mainly for use in implementing the Sort algorithm.) By "interleaved" is meant that if X precedes Y in S1 then X will precede Y in Merge(S1,S2) and similarly for X and Y in S2 (even if S1 or S2 is not in order). The property of stability also holds. See Section 6.1.7 for restrictions on Test and definition of "in order as determined by Test."

See also   Merge, Sort

Implementation

```
   I, J, K, Result : Cell;
begin
  if Test(S2, S1) then
    Result := S2;
    I := Next(S2);
    J := S1;
    K := S2;
    goto Wrong_Loop;
  else
    Result := S1;
    I := Next(S1);
    J := S2;
    K := S1;
    goto Right_Loop;
  end if;
  << Right_Loop >>if Is_End(I) then
    Set_Next(K, J);
    return Result;
  elsif Test(J, I) then
    Attach_To_Tail(K, J);
    J := I;
    I := Next(K);
  else
    K := I;
    Advance(I);
    goto Right_Loop;
  end if;
  << Wrong_Loop >>if Is_End(I) then
    Set_Next(K, J);
    return Result;
  elsif Test(I, J) then
    K := I;
    Advance(I);
    goto Wrong_Loop;
  else
    Attach_To_Tail(K, J);
    J := I;
    I := Next(K);
    goto Right_Loop;
  end if;
end Merge_Non_Empty;
```

7.4.22   MISMATCH

Specification

```
generic
     with function Test(X, Y : Cell) return Boolean;
procedure Mismatch(S1, S2 : in Cell; S3, S4 : out Cell);
```

Description   S1 and S2 are scanned in parallel until the first position is found at which they disagree, using Test as the test for cell equality. S3 and S4 are set to be the subsequences of S1 and S2, respectively, beginning at this disagreement position and going to the end. S1 and S2 are shared.

Time   order $\min(n_1, n_2)m$

Space   0

> where $n_1 = \text{length}(S1)$ and $n_2 = \text{length}(S2)$ and m is the average time for Test

Mutative?   No

Shares?   Yes

Details   Is_End(S3) and Is_End(S4) will both be true if S1 and S2 agree entirely.

See also   Equal

Implementation

```
   To_Be_Done_1 : Cell := S1;
   To_Be_Done_2 : Cell := S2;
 begin
   while not Is_End(To_Be_Done_1)
         and then not Is_End(To_Be_Done_2)
         and then Test(To_Be_Done_1, To_Be_Done_2) loop
     Advance(To_Be_Done_1);
     Advance(To_Be_Done_2);
   end loop;
   S3 := To_Be_Done_1;
   S4 := To_Be_Done_2;
 end Mismatch;
```

7.4.23 NOT_ANY

Specification

```
generic
     with function Test(X : Cell) return Boolean;
function Not_Any(S : Cell)
        return Boolean;
```

Description   Returns true if Test is false of every cell of S, false otherwise. Elements numbered 0, 1, 2, ... are tried in order.

Time   order nm

Space   0

> where $n = $ length(S)and m is the average time for Test

Mutative?   No

Shares?   No

Details   Returns true if Is_End(S) is true.

See also   Every, Some, Not_Every

Implementation

```
   To_Be_Done : Cell := S;
 begin
   while not Is_End(To_Be_Done)
       and then not Test(To_Be_Done) loop
     Advance(To_Be_Done);
   end loop;
   return Is_End(To_Be_Done);
 end Not_Any;
```

7.4.24 NOT_EVERY

Specification

```
generic
     with function Test(X : Cell) return Boolean;
function Not_Every(S : Cell)
        return Boolean;
```

Description   Returns true if Test is false of some cell of S, false otherwise. Elements numbered 0, 1, 2, ... are tried in order.

Time   order nm

Space   0

>   **where** $n = $ length(S)and m is the average time for Test

Mutative?   No

Shares?   No

Details   Returns false if Is_End(S) is true.

See also   Every, Some

Implementation

```
   To_Be_Done : Cell := S;
 begin
   while not Is_End(To_Be_Done)
       and then Test(To_Be_Done) loop
     Advance(To_Be_Done);
   end loop;
   return not Is_End(To_Be_Done);
 end Not_Every;
```

7.4.25 Nth_Rest

Specification

```
function Nth_Rest(N : Integer; S : Cell)
      return Cell;
```

Description   Returns a sequence containing the cells of S numbered N, N+1, ..., Length(S)-1.

Time   order N

Space   order N

Mutative?   No

Shares?   Yes

Details   The numbering of cells begins with 0, hence Nth_Rest(0,S) is the same as S and Nth_Rest(Length(S)-1,S) is the same as Last(S). Assumes that $N \leq \text{Length}(S) - 1$. If $N < 0$, S is returned.

See also   Next, Last

Implementation

```
    To_Be_Done : Cell    := S;
    I          : Integer := N;
begin
  while not Is_End(To_Be_Done) and then I > 0 loop
    I := I - 1;
    Advance(To_Be_Done);
  end loop;
  return To_Be_Done;
end Nth_Rest;
```

7.4.26   POSITION

Specification

```
generic
     with function Test(X : Cell) return Boolean;
function Position(S : Cell)
        return Integer;
```

Description   If S contains an cell X such that Test(X) is true, then the index of the leftmost such item is returned; otherwise -1 is returned.

Time   order nm

Space   0

   where $n = $ length(S)and m is the average time for Test

Mutative?   No

Shares?   No

Details   The index of the first item is 0, of the last is length(S)-1.

See also   Find, Some, Search

Implementation

```
   To_Be_Done : Cell     := S;
   I             : Integer := 0;
 begin
   while not Is_End(To_Be_Done)
       and then not Test(To_Be_Done) loop
     I := I + 1;
     Advance(To_Be_Done);
   end loop;
   if Is_End(To_Be_Done) then
     return -1;
   else
     return I;
   end if;
 end Position;
```

7.4.27 REVERSE_APPEND

Specification

```
function Reverse_Append(S1, S2 : Cell)
       return Cell;
```

Description Returns a sequence consisting of the cells of S1, in reverse order, followed by those of S2 in order. S2 is shared.

Time order n_1

Space order n_1

  where $n_1 = \text{length}(S1)$

Mutative? No

Shares? Yes

See also Reverse_Concatenate, Append

Implementation

```
   Result      : Cell := S2;
   To_Be_Done : Cell := S1;
 begin
   while not Is_End(To_Be_Done) loop
     Result := Copy_Cell(To_Be_Done, Result);
     Advance(To_Be_Done);
   end loop;
   return Result;
 end Reverse_Append;
```

7.4.28   REVERSE_CONCATENATE

Specification

```
function Reverse_Concatenate(S1, S2 : Cell)
       return Cell;
```

Description   Returns a sequence consisting of the cells of S1, in reverse order, followed by those of S2 in order. S1 is mutated and S2 is shared.

Time   order n_1

Space   0

    where $n_1 = \text{length}(S1)$

Mutative?   Yes

Shares?   Yes

See also   Reverse_Append, Append

Implementation

```
   Result    : Cell := S2;
   To_Be_Done : Cell := S1;
   Temp       : Cell;
begin
   while not Is_End(To_Be_Done) loop
     Temp := To_Be_Done;
     Advance(To_Be_Done);
     Set_Next(Temp, Result);
     Result := Temp;
   end loop;
   return Result;
end Reverse_Concatenate;
```

7.4.29 SEARCH

Specification

```
generic
    with function Test(X, Y : Cell) return Boolean;
function Search(S1, S2 : Cell)
      return Cell;
```

Description   Returns the leftmost occurrence of a subsequence in S2 that matches S1 cell for cell, using Test as the the test for cell equality. If no matching subsequence is found, a sequence S is returned such that Is_End(S) is true.

Time   order nm

Space   0

> **where** $n = $ length(S)and m is the average time for Test

Mutative?   No

Shares?   Yes

See also   Position, Find, Some, Search

Implementation

```
    To_Be_Done      : Cell := S2;
    Tail_1, Tail_2 : Cell;
    procedure Mismatch_Aux is new Mismatch(Test);
  begin
    loop
      Mismatch_Aux(S1, To_Be_Done, Tail_1, Tail_2);
      if Is_End(Tail_1) then
        return To_Be_Done;
      elsif Is_End(Tail_2) then
        return Tail_2;
      end if;
      Advance(To_Be_Done);
    end loop;
  end Search;
```

7.4.30 SOME

Specification

```
generic
      with function Test(X : Cell) return Boolean;
function Some(S : Cell)
        return Boolean;
```

Description   Returns true if Test is true of some cell of S, false otherwise. Elements numbered 0, 1, 2, ... are tried in order.

Time   order nm

Space   0

   where $n = $ length(S)and m is the average time for Test

Mutative?   No

Shares?   No

Details   Returns false if Is_End(S) is true.

See also   Not_Every, Every, Not_Any

Implementation

```
   To_Be_Done : Cell := S;
 begin
   while not Is_End(To_Be_Done)
       and then not Test(To_Be_Done) loop
     Advance(To_Be_Done);
   end loop;
   return not Is_End(To_Be_Done);
 end Some;
```

7.4.31 SORT

Specification

```
generic
      Log_Of_Max_Num : Integer;
  Empty           : Cell;
  with function Test(X, Y : Cell) return Boolean;
function Sort(S : Cell)
        return Cell;
```

Description Returns a sequence containing the same cells as S, but in order as determined by Test. S is mutated.

Time   order $(n \log n)m$

Space   0

  where $n = \text{length}(S)$and m is the average time for Test

Mutative?   Yes

Shares?   No

Details   This is a stable sorting algorithm. See Section 6.1.7 for restrictions on Test and definition of "in order as determined by Test."

See also   Merge

Implementation

```
-- Merge-sort algorithm, using "register adder" technique
  type Table is array(0 .. Log_Of_Max_Num) of Cell;
  Register                     : Table    := (others => Empty);
  I, Maximum_Bit_Position : Integer := 0;
  To_Be_Done                   : Cell     := S;
  Bit, Carry                   : Cell;
  function Merge_Aux is new Merge_Non_Empty(Test);
begin
  while not (Is_End(To_Be_Done)) loop
    Carry := To_Be_Done;
    Advance(To_Be_Done);
    Set_Next(Carry, Empty);
    I := 0;
    loop
      Bit := Register(I);
      exit when Is_End(Bit);
      Carry := Merge_Aux(Bit, Carry);
      Register(I) := Empty;
      I := I + 1;
    end loop;
    Register(I) := Carry;
    if Maximum_Bit_Position < I then
      Maximum_Bit_Position := I;
    end if;
  end loop;
  Carry := Register(I);
  loop
    I := I + 1;
    exit when I > Maximum_Bit_Position;
    Bit := Register(I);
    if not Is_End(Bit) then
      Carry := Merge_Aux(Bit, Carry);
    end if;
  end loop;
  return Carry;
end Sort;
```

8

Using the Packages

8.1 Partially instantiated packages

The purpose of each of these packages, called "PIPs" is to plug together
a low-level data abstraction package with a structural or representational
abstraction package, while leaving the `Element` type (and perhaps other
parameters) generic. Here we only show PIPs obtained from combining
each of the three low-level representations with the `Singly_Linked_Lists`
structural abstraction. (There are twelve PIPs included in this release of
the library.)

8.1.1 USING SYSTEM ALLOCATED SINGLY LINKED

From file saslpip.ada--

```
with System_Allocated_Singly_Linked, Singly_Linked_Lists;
generic
   type Element is private;
package System_Allocated_Singly_Linked_Lists is

   package Low_Level is
       new System_Allocated_Singly_Linked(Element);
   use  Low_Level;

   package Inner is
    new Singly_Linked_Lists(Element, Sequence, Nil, First,
          Next, Construct, Set_First, Set_Next, Free);

end System_Allocated_Singly_Linked_Lists;--
```

8.1.2 USING USER ALLOCATED SINGLY LINKED

From file uaslpip.ada--

```
with User_Allocated_Singly_Linked, Singly_Linked_Lists;
generic
   Heap_Size : in Natural;
   type Element is private;
package User_Allocated_Singly_Linked_Lists is
```

```
package Low_Level is
  new User_Allocated_Singly_Linked(Heap_Size, Element);
use  Low_Level;

package Inner is
  new Singly_Linked_Lists(Element, Sequence, Nil, First,
       Next, Construct, Set_First, Set_Next, Free);

end User_Allocated_Singly_Linked_Lists;--
```

8.1.3   USING AUTO REALLOCATING SINGLY LINKED

From file arslpip.ada--

```
with Auto_Reallocating_Singly_Linked;
with Singly_Linked_Lists;
generic

  Initial_Number_Of_Blocks : in Positive;
  Block_Size               : in Positive;
  Coefficient              : in Float;
  type Element is private;

package Auto_Reallocating_Singly_Linked_Lists is

  package Low_Level is new
      Auto_Reallocating_Singly_Linked(
          Initial_Number_Of_Blocks, Block_Size,
          Coefficient, Element);
  use  Low_Level;

  package Inner is
   new Singly_Linked_Lists(Element, Sequence, Nil, First,
        Next, Construct, Set_First, Set_Next, Free);

end Auto_Reallocating_Singly_Linked_Lists;
```

8.2   Integer instantiation

A PIP can then be used by instantiating the Element type and any other remaining generic parameters. For example:

```
with System_Allocated_Singly_Linked_Lists;
package Integer_Linked is
  new System_Allocated_Singly_Linked_Lists(Integer);
```

Note that the **Inner** package of an instance of a PIP must be **use**d in order to make available all of the subprogram names and other identifiers of the package without requiring a prefix, as in

```
with Integer_Linked;
procedure Application is
  use Integer_Linked.Inner;
    . . .
```

8.3   Test suite and output

Using **Integer_Linked**, a test suite is produced from the test suite package skeleton given in Chapter 6 and the examples given with each subprogram.

The output that is produced is indicated in the comments in those examples.

Part II

Restricted-Access Data Structures

9

Introduction

The singly-linked-list data structure provided in Part 1 offers great versatility in what can be programmed, but that versatility has a drawback: there is little to prevent the programmer from creating application code that exhibits certain insidious errors, such as unintentional circularities in lists that cause programs to loop indefinitely. But we can build upon the singly-linked-list structure and restrict the kinds of operations upon it, using data abstraction, providing security against some kinds of errors. Thus, aside from potentially providing greater efficiency in the situations in which they can be used, the three linear data structures provided in this part may be a better choice than direct use of singly-linked lists, especially for less experienced programmers.

The following packages are included in this part:

- `Double_Ended_Lists` employs header cells with singly-linked lists to make some operations such as concatenation more efficient and to provide more security in various computations with lists.

- `Stacks` provides the familiar linear data structure in which insertions and deletions are restricted to one end.

- `Output_Restricted_Deques` provides a data structure that restricts insertions to both ends and deletions to one end.

These three packages are representational abstractions that produce different structural abstractions from different representations of sequences. For example, any of the three different low-level representations of singly-linked lists provided in Part 1 (Chapters 3, 4, 5) can easily be plugged together with `Double_Ended_Lists` to produce three different versions of this data structure and its associated algorithms. Each version is provided in the library as a Partially Instantiated Package (PIP), which is a generic package with only the element type, and perhaps some configuration parameters, as generic parameters. See Chapter 13 for further details on the form and usage of PIPs.

Similarly, three more PIPs are provided for plugging together each of the low-level representations of singly-linked lists with `Stacks`. The `Stacks` package can also be combined with low-level representations other than linked lists, since the generic parameters of these packages do not need all of the characteristics of linked-lists (in particular, no `Set_Next` operation is needed). As an illustration of this, Appendix B shows how to supply the needed low-level operations using a simple vector representation.

The parameterization of `Output_Restricted_Deques` is such that the operations assumed are easily provided by `Double_Ended_Lists`. Thus we obtain PIPs by plugging together each of the three PIPs for `Double_Ended_-Lists` with with `Output_Restricted_Deques`, producing three different versions of that data structure and its operations. One could, however, produce other versions in terms of a vector representation, since the operations assumed as parameters for `Output_Restricted_Deques`, like those of `Stacks`, can also be efficiently performed in terms of a vector representation.

10

Double Ended Lists Package

10.1 Overview

This package creates a data type called `Del` and provides 47 subprograms for manipulating values of this type. Basically `Del`s are finite sequences and the operations provided are similar to to those of `Singly_Linked_-Lists` (Chapter 6), but some operations such as concatenation are more efficient (constant time rather than linear in the length of the arguments). In addition, more security against certain kinds of semantic errors is provided, since the package user does not have direct access to pointer values. For example, with `Singly_Linked_Lists` it is possible using the `Set_Next` operation to create a circular list, causing other operations to loop indefinitely, but this is not possible with `Del`s.

The package is generic in the type of elements stored and in the subprograms that provide operations on a singly-linked-list representation of finite sequences. This is a representational abstraction package in which the parameterization is the same as that for `Singly_Linked_Lists`, so that any low-level representation package that can be plugged together with `Singly_Linked_Lists` can also be plugged together with `Double_Ended_-Lists`.

10.1.1 A MODEL OF DOUBLE-ENDED-LISTS

The internal representation of the `Del` type is as a record containing three pointers into a singly-linked-list representation of a sequence: first-element, last-element, and current-element. While this representation is not directly accessible to the package user, it is nonetheless useful to think in terms of the three pointers as a model of double-ended-lists, both for understanding of what the operations do and of how to use them most effectively.

- The first-element pointer gives the same kind of access to a sequence as one has with `Singly_Linked_Lists`.

- The last-element pointer makes it possible to access the last element in constant time, rather than having to traverse the sequence, and consequently concatenation of two sequences can be done in constant time.

- The current-element pointer is used as a marker within the sequence; many of the subprograms operate only on the elements starting with

the current element through the end of the sequence, and some of
these convey their result by moving the current-element pointer to a
new position (always to the right).

10.1.2 INVARIANTS

The user of **Double_Ended_Lists** does not have direct access to any of
the three pointers; only through certain subprograms can changes in these
pointers be effected. The main consequence of this fact, and of the selection of operations actually provided, is that certain properties (called
invariants) of the representation are maintained, which in turn implies
that certain kinds of errors are ruled out. These invariants are as follows:
For each value of type **Del**, there is a finite sequence such that either the
sequence is empty, in which case the generic formal subprogram **Is_End**
returns true on all three pointers; or, letting the sequence be

$$x_0, x_1, \ldots, x_{n-1},$$

1. There is a sequence of pointers

$$p_0, p_1, \ldots, p_n$$

   such that p_i points to x_i for $i = 0, \ldots, n - 1$; $p_i = \text{Next}(p_{i-1})$ for
   $i = 1, \ldots, n$; and **Is_End**(p_n) is true.

2. The first-element pointer equals p_0.

3. The last-element pointer equals p_{n-1}.

4. The current-element pointer equals p_i for some i, $i = 0, \ldots, n$.

A direct consequence of these invariants is that there can be no loops in
double-ended lists, unlike the case with **Singly_Linked_Lists**.
    Note that possibly **Is_End** is true of the current-element pointer. In this
case we say that the current-element pointer is *off the end* of the sequence.

10.1.3 CLASSIFICATION OF OPERATIONS

As is the case with **Singly_Linked_Lists**, the operations on **Double_-
Ended_Lists** can be classified as follows:

1. Construction and modification of sequences

2. Examination of sequences

3. Computing with sequences

The following three subsections give a brief overview of these categories, leaving the details and examples of usage to the individual subprogram descriptions. In comparison with the selection of operations on **Singly_-Linked_Lists**, the operations on **Double_Ended_Lists** differ in the following general ways:

- Construction, modification, and examination of sequences includes operations that take advantage of the last-element and current-element pointers.

- Many of the operations operate on the current element or on all of the elements from the current element to the end.

- There are no operations like **Set_Next** that permit pointers to be changed to arbitrary values.

- There is no sharing of list structure.

- Construction and modification operations are provided as procedures rather than functions, and there are no **Copy** versions of the operations, since it is expected that in most cases **Del**s will be treated as objects on which computation will be performed by modification.

The **Del** type is a limited private type, and thus assignment from one variable of type **Del** to another is prohibited by the language rules. There is, however, a **Copy_Sequence** operation that can be used in place of assignment.

10.1.4   CONSTRUCTION AND MODIFICATION OF SEQUENCES

All of the operations in this category are procedures.

Basic construction

Declaration of a variable to be of type **Del** initializes the variable to represent an empty sequence. There are three operations for adding a single element to a sequence: **Add_First(The_Element, S)**, **Add_Last(The_-Element, S)**, and **Add_Current(The_Element, S)**.

Copy_Sequence(S1, S2) produces a copy of sequence S2 in S1 that does not overlap with S2 in its memory representation.

Basic Modification

Set_First(S, E) changes S so that its first element is E but the following elements are unchanged. Similarly, Set_Last(S, E) and Set_Current(S, E) change the last and current elements, respectively. Advance(S) moves the current-element pointer one element forward. Initialize(S) resets the current-element pointer to the first element.

Drop_Head(S) removes the elements of S from the first element up to and including the current element. The complementary operation **Drop_-Tail(S)** removes the elements beyond the current element. **Free(S)** removes all the elements; its use is to return the cells occupied by S to the available space pool. The header cell is retained, but is made empty.

Reversing

There is one operation for reversing the order of elements in a sequence: **Invert(S)**.

Splitting and Concatenation

Split(S1, S2) splits S1 into two parts: all elements up to and including its current element (this becomes the new value of S1) and all elements following the current element of S1 (this becomes the new value of S2). The old value of S2 is lost (the cells it occupies are returned to available space). The current element of the new S1 its last element and of the new S2 is the first element.

Conversely, **Concatenate(S1, S2)** modifies S1 to be the concatenation of its input value and S2. The output value of S2 is made empty. The current element of the new S1 is the same as in the input value.

Thus, if S2 is empty, the net effect of

$$\text{Split(S1, S2); Concatenate(S1, S2);}$$

is a no-op. (If S2 is non-empty the effect is the same as that of **Free(S2)**.)

Merging and Sorting

Merge(S1, S2) modifies S1 to be a sequence containing the same elements as the input values of S1 and S2, interleaved. If S1 and S2 are in order as determined by its generic parameter **Test**, then the result will be also.

By "interleaved" is meant that if X precedes Y in S1 then X will precede Y in the new S1 and similarly for X and Y in S2 (even if S1 or S2 is not in order). See Section 6.1.7 for discussion of the restrictions on Test and definition of "in order as determined by Test.""

Sort(S) takes a comparison function **Test** and modifies S to be a sequence containing the same elements as S, but in order as determined by **Test**.

Both **Merge** and **Sort** are *stable*: elements considered equal by **Test** (see the discussion in Section 6.1.7) will remain in their original order.

Deletion and substitution

There are four different operations for deleting elements from a sequence, all of which have a generic parameter **Test(X)** or **Test(X,Y)**, which are **Boolean** valued functions on element values X and Y. For example, **Delete_-If(S)** modifies S by removing those elements E of the input value of S that

satisfy Test(E) = True. See also Delete, Delete_If_Not, and Delete_-
Duplicates.

Similarly, there are three generic subprograms for substituting a new ele-
ment for some of the elements in a sequence: Substitute(New_Item, Old_-
Item, S), Substitute_If(New_Item, S), and Substitute_If_Not(New_-
Item, S).

10.1.5 EXAMINING SEQUENCES

All of the operations in this category are functions, except Mismatch,
Find, Find_If, Find_If_Not and Search.

Basic queries

Is_End(S) returns the Boolean value True if the current-element pointer
of S is off the end, False otherwise. Is_Empty(S) returns True if S has
no elements, False otherwise. Length(S) returns the number of elements
in S. First(S), Last(S), and Current(S) return the first, last, and current elements of a non-empty sequence S; if S is empty they all apply the
generic formal parameter First to a Sequence with no elements, raising
an exception.

Counting

The remaining operations for examining sequences are generic, all having
either Test(X) or Test(X, Y) as a generic parameter. For example, Count,
Count_If, and Count_If_Not are Integer valued functions for counting the
elements in a sequence satisfying or not satisfying Test.

Equality and matching

Equal(S1, S2) returns true if S1 and S2 contain the same elements, beginning with their current elements, in the same order, using Test as the test
for the element equality. Using "=" for Test one obtains the ordinary check
for equality of two sequences, but this function can be used to extend other
equivalence relations on elements to an equivalence relation on sequences.

A more general operation is the procedure Mismatch(S1, S2), which
scans the input values of S1 and S2 in parallel until the first position is
found at which they disagree, again starting with the current elements and
using Test as the test for element equality. Mismatch modifies the current-
element pointers of S1 and S2 to be the subsequences of its inputs beginning
at the disagreement position and going to the end.

Searching

There are eight operations for searching a sequence. If S contains an element
E such that Test(Item,E) is true, at or to the right of its current-element
pointer, then Find(Item, S) moves the current-element pointer of S to

the the leftmost such element; otherwise the current-element pointer is moved off the end of S. Find_If and Find_If_Not are related procedures. Search(S1, S2) searches S2, starting with the current element, for the leftmost occurrence of a subsequence that element-wise matches S1, and moves the current-element pointer of S2 to this subsequence. If no matching subsequence is found, the current element pointer of S2 is set off the end.

The other operations for searching are all Boolean valued functions. Some(S) returns True if Test is true of some element of S, false otherwise. Similarly, Every(S) checks if Test is true of every element of S, Not_-Every(S) checks if Test is false for some element, and Not_Any(S) checks if Test is false for every element. All of these operations start with the current element and proceed to the right, just through the first element that determines the answer (e.g., if S from its current element to the end is a sequence of integers 2, 3, 5, 7, 11, the operation is Some, and Test(X) checks for X being odd, then Test is performed only on 2 and 3).

10.1.6   COMPUTING WITH SEQUENCES

Procedural iteration

The five functions and procedures in this category are generic subprograms for iterating over a sequence, applying some given subprogram to each element. For_Each, for example, is a procedure that takes a generic parameter called The_Procedure; For_Each(S) computes The_Procedure(E) for each element E of S, starting with the current element and going to the end. For_Each_2 takes two sequences and a procedure with two arguments and applies the procedure to corresponding pairs of elements in the sequences, starting with their current elements.

Mapping

Map(S) modifies S to consist of the results of applying its generic parameter F to each element of S, from the current element to the end. F must be a function from the Element type to the Element type. Map_2 is a similar procedure for application of a function F of two arguments to corresponding pairs of elements of two sequences S1 and S2.

Reduction

Reduce applies a function of two arguments, F(X, Y), to reduce a sequence to a single value; for example, if F is "+", Reduce(S) sums up the elements of S. The elements included in the reduction are those from the current element of S to the end. It is also necessary to supply Reduce with an element that is the identity for F; e.g., 0 in the case of "+" when the elements are integers.

10.2   Package specification

The package specification is as follows:

```
generic

   type Element  is private;
   type Sequence is private;
   Nil : Sequence;
   with function First(S : Sequence) return Element;
   with function Next(S : Sequence) return Sequence;
   with function Construct(E : Element; S : Sequence)
       return Sequence;
   with procedure Set_First(S : Sequence; E : Element);
   with procedure Set_Next(S1, S2 : Sequence);
   with procedure Free_Construct(S : Sequence);

package Double_Ended_Lists is

   type Del is limited private;

  {The subprogram specifications}

private

   type Del is record
     First   : Sequence := Nil;
     Current : Sequence := Nil;
     Last    : Sequence := Nil;
   end record;

end Double_Ended_Lists;
```

10.3   Package body

The package body is as follows:

```
with Singly_Linked_Lists;
package body Double_Ended_Lists is

   package Regular_Lists is
       new Singly_Linked_Lists(Element, Sequence, Nil,
           First, Next, Construct, Set_First,
           Set_Next, Free_Construct);
```

```ada
procedure Make_Empty(S : out Del) is
begin
  S.First := Nil;
  S.Current := Nil;
  S.Last := Nil;
end Make_Empty;
pragma Inline(Make_Empty);

procedure Put_List(S : out Del; L : Sequence) is
begin
  S.First := L;
  S.Current := L;
  S.Last := Regular_Lists.Last(L);
end Put_List;
pragma Inline(Put_List);

{The subprogram bodies}

end Double_Ended_Lists;
```

10.4   Definitions for the examples

The following definitions are referenced in the examples included in the subprogram descriptions. (This is the skeleton of a test suite in which the examples are included.)

```ada
with Double_Ended_Lists_1; -- a PIP;
package Integer_Double_Ended_Lists is
  new Double_Ended_Lists_1(Integer);

with Integer_Double_Ended_Lists, Text_Io, Examples_Help;
procedure Test_Del is
  use Integer_Double_Ended_Lists.Inner, Text_Io,
    Examples_Help;
  Flag : Boolean := True;

  function Shuffle_Test(X, Y : Integer) return Boolean is
  begin
    Flag := not Flag;
    return Flag;
  end Shuffle_Test;

  procedure Iota(N : Integer; Result : in out Del) is
  begin
    for I in 0 .. N - 1 loop
```

```
      Add_Last(I, Result);
    end loop;
  end Iota;

  procedure Show_List(S : Del) is
    procedure Show_List_Aux is
        new For_Each(Print_Integer);
  begin
    Put("--:"); Show_List_Aux(S); New_Line;
  end Show_List;

begin

  {Examples from the subprograms}


  Show("End Of Tests");
end;
```

10.5 Subprograms

10.5.1 ADD_CURRENT

Specification

```
procedure Add_Current(The_Element: Element; S: in out Del);
pragma inline(Add_Current);
```

Description   Inserts The_Element in S after the current element.

Time   constant

Space   constant

Mutative?   Yes

Shares?   No

Details   The current element is unchanged. Attempts to apply Next to the current element pointer even if Is_End is true of this pointer.

See also   Add_First, Add_Last

Examples

```
declare
  Temp : Del;
begin
  Iota(3, Temp);
  Add_Current(5, Temp);
  Show_List(Temp);
-- 0  5  1  2
  Add_Current(6, Temp);
  Show_List(Temp);
-- 0  6  5  1  2
end;
```

Implementation

```
    Next_One, New_One : Sequence;
  begin
    Next_One := Next(S.Current);
    New_One := Construct(The_Element, Next_One);
    Set_Next(S.Current, New_One);
    if Regular_Lists.Is_End(Next_One) then
      S.Last := New_One;
    end if;
  end Add_Current;
```

10.5.2   ADD_FIRST

Specification

```
procedure Add_First(The_Element : Element; S : in out Del);
pragma inline(Add_First);
```

Description   Inserts The_Element as the first element of S.

Time   constant

Space   constant

Mutative?   Yes

Shares?   No

Details   The current element is unchanged, unless S was empty.

See also   Add_Current, Add_Last

Examples

```
declare
  Temp : Del;
begin
  Iota(3, Temp);
  Add_First(5, Temp);
  Initialize(Temp);
  Show_List(Temp);
-- 5  0  1  2
end;
```

Implementation

```
begin
  S.First := Construct(The_Element, S.First);
  if Regular_Lists.Is_End(S.Last) then
    S.Last := S.First;
    Initialize(S);
  end if;
end Add_First;
```

10.5.3 ADD_LAST

Specification

```
procedure Add_Last(The_Element : Element; S : in out Del);
pragma inline(Add_Last);
```

Description   Inserts The_Element as the last element of S.

Time   constant

Space   constant

Mutative?   Yes

Shares?   No

Details   The current element is unchanged, unless S was empty.

See also   Add_Current, Add_First

Examples

```
declare
  Temp : Del;
begin
  Iota(3, Temp);
  Add_Last(5, Temp);
  Show_List(Temp);
-- 0  1  2  5
end;
```

Implementation

```
  Temp : Sequence := S.Last;
begin
  S.Last := Construct(The_Element, Nil);
  if Regular_Lists.Is_End(Temp) then
    S.First := S.Last;
    Initialize(S);
  else
    Set_Next(Temp, S.Last);
  end if;
end Add_Last;
```

10.5.4 ADVANCE

Specification

```
procedure Advance(S : in out Del);
pragma inline(Advance);
```

Description   Moves the current element pointer one element to the right.

Time   constant

Space   0

Mutative?   No

Shares?   No

Details   Tries to apply the Next function to the current element pointer even if Is_End is true of this pointer.

See also

Implementation

```
begin
  S.Current := Next(S.Current);
end Advance;
```

10.5.5 CONCATENATE

Specification

```
procedure Concatenate(S1, S2 : in out Del);
pragma inline(Concatenate);
```

Description   S1 is modified to be the concatenation of its input value and S2.

Time   constant

Space   0

Mutative?   Yes

Shares?   No

Details   The output value of S2 is made empty. The current element of the new S1 is the same as in the input value.

See also

Examples

```
declare
  Temp_1, Temp_2 : Del;
begin
  Iota(5, Temp_1);
  Iota(6, Temp_2);
  Concatenate(Temp_1, Temp_2);
  Show_List(Temp_1);
--  0  1  2  3  4  0  1  2  3  4  5
end;
declare
  Temp_1, Temp_2 : Del;
begin
  Iota(6, Temp_2);
  Concatenate(Temp_1, Temp_2);
  Show_List(Temp_1);
--  0  1  2  3  4  5
end;
declare
  Temp_1, Temp_2 : Del;
begin
  Iota(5, Temp_1);
  Concatenate(Temp_1, Temp_2);
  Show_List(Temp_1);
```

```
--  0  1  2  3  4
end;
```

Implementation

```
begin
  if Is_Empty(S1) then
    S1 := S2;
    Make_Empty(S2);
  elsif not Is_Empty(S2) then
    Set_Next(S1.Last, S2.First);
    S1.Last := S2.Last;
    Make_Empty(S2);
  end if;
end Concatenate;
```

10.5.6   COPY_SEQUENCE

Specification

```
procedure Copy_Sequence(S1 : out Del; S2 : Del);
```

Description   S1 is made to be a copy of S2.

Time   order n_2

Space   order n_2

>   **where** $n_2 = $ length(S2)

Mutative?   No

Shares?   No

Details   The current element of S1 becomes the first element (and thus may differ from the current element of S2).

See also

Examples

```
declare
  Temp_1, Temp_2 : Del;
begin
  Iota(3, Temp_1);
  Copy_Sequence(Temp_2, Temp_1);
  Show_List(Temp_2);
--  0  1  2
end;
```

Implementation

```
  Temp : Sequence := Regular_Lists.Copy_Sequence(S2.First);
begin
  S1.First := Temp;
  S1.Current := Temp;
  S1.Last := Regular_Lists.Last(Temp);
end Copy_Sequence;
```

10.5.7   COUNT

Specification

```
generic
  with function Test(X, Y : Element) return Boolean;
function Count(Item : Element; S : Del)
    return Integer;
```

Description   Returns a non-negative integer equal to the number of elements E of S such that Test(Item,E) is true, starting with the current element.

Time   order nm

Space   0

>   **where** $n = \text{length(S)}$ and m is the average time for Test

Mutative?   No

Shares?   No

See also   Count_If, Count_If_Not, Find

Examples

```
declare
  Temp : Del;
  function Count_When_Divides is new
    Integer_Double_Ended_Lists.Inner.Count(Test=>Divides);
begin
  Iota(10, Temp);
  Show_Integer(Count_When_Divides(3, Temp));
--  4
end;
```

Implementation

```
   function Count_Aux is new Regular_Lists.Count(Test);
begin
  return Count_Aux(Item, S.Current);
end Count;
```

10.5.8   COUNT_IF

Specification

```
generic
     with function Test(X : Element) return Boolean;
function Count_If(S : Del)
     return Integer;
```

Description   Returns a non-negative integer equal to the number of elements E of S such that Test(E) is true, starting with the current element.

Time   order nm

Space   0

where $n = $ length(S)and m is the average time for Test

Mutative?   No

Shares?   No

See also   Count, Count_If_Not, Find, Find_If

Examples

```
declare
  Temp : Del;
  function Count_If_Odd is new Count_If(Test => Odd);
begin
  Iota(9, Temp);
  Show_Integer(Count_If_Odd(Temp));
--   4
end;
```

Implementation

```
   function Count_Aux is new Regular_Lists.Count_If(Test);
begin
  return Count_Aux(S.Current);
end Count_If;
```

10.5.9   COUNT_IF_NOT

Specification

```
generic
      with function Test(X : Element) return Boolean;
function Count_If_Not(S : Del)
        return Integer;
```

Description   Returns a non-negative integer equal to the number of elements E of S such that Test(E) is false, starting with the current element.

Time   order nm

Space   0

>   **where** $n = $ length(S)and m is the average time for Test

Mutative?   No

Shares?   No

See also   Count, Count_If, Find, Find_If_Not

Examples

```
declare
  Temp : Del;
  function Count_If_Not_Odd is
      new Count_If_Not(Test => Odd);
begin
  Iota(9, Temp);
  Show_Integer(Count_If_Not_Odd(Temp));
--   5
end;
```

Implementation

```
   function Count_Aux is new Regular_Lists.Count_If_Not(Test);
begin
  return Count_Aux(S.Current);
end Count_If_Not;
```

10.5.10 CURRENT

Specification

```
function Current(S : Del)
       return Element;
pragma inline(Current);
```

Description   Returns the current element of S.

Time   constant

Space   0

Mutative?   No

Shares?   No

Details   If the current element pointer of S is off the end, this function will apply First to a Sequence with no elements, raising an exception.

See also

Implementation

```
begin
  return First(S.Current);
end Current;
```

10.5.11   DELETE

Specification

```
generic
      with function Test(X, Y : Element) return Boolean;
procedure Delete(Item : Element; S : in out Del);
```

Description   Modifies S by deleting all elements E of S for which Test(Item, E) is true.

Time   order nm

Space   0

  where $n = $ length(S)and m is the average time for Test

Mutative?   Yes

Shares?   No

See also   Delete_If, Delete_If_Not, Delete_Duplicates

Examples

```
declare
  Temp : Del;
  procedure Delete_When_Divides is new
    Integer_Double_Ended_Lists.Inner.Delete(Test=>Divides);
begin
  Iota(15, Temp);
  Delete_When_Divides(3, Temp);
  Show_List(Temp);
--   1  2  4  5  7  8  10  11  13  14
end;
```

Implementation

```
   function Delete_Aux is new Regular_Lists.Delete(Test);
begin
  Put_List(S, Delete_Aux(Item, S.First));
end Delete;
```

10.5.12   DELETE_DUPLICATES

Specification

```
generic
      with function Test(X, Y : Element) return Boolean;
   procedure Delete_Duplicates(S : in out Del);
```

Description   Modifies S by deleting all duplicated occurrences of elements, using Test as the test for equality.

Time   order $n^2 m$

Space   0

where $n = $ length(S)and m is the average time for Test

Mutative?   Yes

Shares?   No

Details   The left-most occurrence of each duplicated element is retained.

See also   Delete, Delete_If

Examples

```
declare
   Temp : Del;
   procedure Delete_Duplicates_When_Divides is
       new Delete_Duplicates(Test=>Divides);
begin
   Iota(20, Temp);
   Advance(Temp);
   Drop_Head(Temp);
   Delete_Duplicates_When_Divides(Temp);
   Show_List(Temp);
--   2  3  5  7  11  13  17  19
end;
```

Implementation

```
   function Delete_Aux is
       new Regular_Lists.Delete_Duplicates(Test);
begin
   Put_List(S, Delete_Aux(S.First));
end Delete_Duplicates;
```

10.5.13   DELETE_IF

Specification

```
generic
      with function Test(X : Element) return Boolean;
procedure Delete_If(S : in out Del);
```

Description   Modifies S by deleting all elements E for which Test(E) is true.

Time   order nm

Space   order n

   where $n = $ length(S)and m is the average time for Test

Mutative?   Yes

Shares?   No

See also   Delete, Delete_If_Not

Examples

```
declare
  Temp : Del;
  procedure Delete_If_Odd is new Delete_If(Test => Odd);
begin
  Iota(10, Temp);
  Delete_If_Odd(Temp);
  Show_List(Temp);
--   0  2  4  6  8
end;
```

Implementation

```
   function Delete_Aux is new Regular_Lists.Delete_If(Test);
begin
  Put_List(S, Delete_Aux(S.First));
end Delete_If;
```

10.5.14   DELETE_IF_NOT

Specification

```
generic
     with function Test(X : Element) return Boolean;
procedure Delete_If_Not(S : in out Del);
```

Description   Modifies S by deleting all elements E for which Test(E) is false.

Time   order nm

Space   order n

> **where** $n =$ length(S)and m is the average time for Test

Mutative?   Yes

Shares?   No

See also   Delete, Delete_If

Examples

```
declare
  Temp : Del;
  procedure Delete_If_Not_Odd is
      new Delete_If_Not(Test => Odd);
begin
  Iota(10, Temp);
  Delete_If_Not_Odd(Temp);
  Show_List(Temp);
--   1  3  5  7  9
end;
```

Implementation

```
   function Delete_Aux is
       new Regular_Lists.Delete_If_Not(Test);
begin
  Put_List(S, Delete_Aux(S.First));
end Delete_If_Not;
```

10.5.15   DROP_HEAD

Specification

```
procedure Drop_Head(S : in out Del);
pragma inline(Drop_Head);
```

Description   S is modified by removing all elements up to and including the current element.

Time   order k

Space   0

   where k is the number of elements up to and including the current element.

Mutative?   Yes

Shares?   No

Details   The elements removed are returned to the storage allocator. If Is_End is true of the current element or the current element is the last element, all elements of S are removed.

See also

Examples

```
declare
  Temp : Del;
begin
  Iota(4, Temp);
  Advance(Temp);
  Drop_Head(Temp);
  Show_List(Temp);
--   2  3
end;
```

Implementation

```
   Next_One : Sequence;
begin
   if Is_End(S) then
     Regular_Lists.Free_Sequence(S.First);
     Make_Empty(S);
   else
     Next_One := Next(S.Current);
     if Regular_Lists.Is_End(Next_One) then
       Regular_Lists.Free_Sequence(S.First);
       Make_Empty(S);
     else
       Set_Next(S.Current, Nil);
       Regular_Lists.Free_Sequence(S.First);
       S.First := Next_One;
       Initialize(S);
     end if;
   end if;
end Drop_Head;
```

10.5.16   DROP_TAIL

Specification

```
procedure Drop_Tail(S : in out Del);
pragma inline(Drop_Tail);
```

Description   S is modified by removing all elements following the current element.

Time   order k

Space   0

>   **where** k = the number of elements following the current element

Mutative?   Yes

Shares?   No

Details   The elements removed are returned to the storage allocator. If Is_End is true of the current element or the current element is the last element, no elements of S are removed.

See also   Drop_Head

Examples

```
declare
  Temp : Del;
begin
  Iota(4, Temp);
  Advance(Temp);
  Drop_Tail(Temp);
  Initialize(Temp);
  Show_List(Temp);
-- 0  1
end;
```

Implementation

```
   Next_One : Sequence;
begin
  if not Is_End(S) then
    Next_One := Next(S.Current);
    if not Regular_Lists.Is_End(Next_One) then
      Set_Next(S.Current, Nil);
      Regular_Lists.Free_Sequence(Next_One);
      S.Last := S.Current;
    end if;
  end if;
end Drop_Tail;
```

10.5.17   EQUAL

Specification

```
generic
     with function Test(X, Y : Element) return Boolean;
function Equal(S1, S2: Del)
     return Boolean;
```

Description   Returns true if S1 and S2 contain the same elements in the same order, starting with their current elements and using Test as the test for element equality.

Time   order $m \min(\text{length}(S1), \text{length}(S2))$

Space   0

   where m is the average time for Test

Mutative?   No

Shares?   No

See also   Mismatch

Implementation

```
   function Equal_Aux is new Regular_Lists.Equal(Test);
begin
   return Equal_Aux(S1.Current, S2.Current);
end Equal;
```

10.5.18 EVERY

Specification

```
generic
     with function Test(X : Element) return Boolean;
function Every(S : Del)
        return Boolean;
```

Description   Returns true if Test is true of every element of S from the current element to the end, false otherwise. Elements starting with the current element and in successively higher positions are considered in order.

Time   order nm

Space   0

where $n = $ length(S)and m is the average time for Test

Mutative?   No

Shares?   No

Details   Returns true if the current pointer of S is off the end.

See also   Not_Every, Some

Examples

```
declare
  Temp : Del;
  function Every_Odd is new Every(Test => Odd);
begin
  Iota(10, Temp);
  Show_Boolean(Every_Odd(Temp));
--  False
end;
declare
  Temp : Del;
  function Every_Odd is new Every(Test => Odd);
  procedure Delete_If_Not_Odd is
      new Delete_If_Not(Test => Odd);
begin
  Iota(10, Temp);
  Delete_If_Not_Odd(Temp);
  Show_Boolean(Every_Odd(Temp));
--  True
end;
```

Implementation

```
    function Every_Aux is new Regular_Lists.Every(Test);
begin
    return Every_Aux(S.Current);
end Every;
```

10.5.19   FIND

Specification

```
generic
      with function Test(X, Y : Element) return Boolean;
   procedure Find(Item : Element; S : in out Del);
```

Description   If S contains an element E such that Test(Item,E) is true, at the current element or beyond, then the leftmost such element is made to be the current element; otherwise the current element pointer falls off the end of S.

Time   order nm

Space   0

   where $n = $ length(S)and m is the average time for Test

Mutative?   No

Shares?   No

See also   Find_If, Find_If_Not, Some, Search

Examples

```
declare
  Temp : Del;
  procedure Find_When_Greater is new Find(Test => "<");
begin
  Iota(20, Temp);
  Find_When_Greater(9, Temp);
  Show_List(Temp);
--   10   11   12   13   14   15   16   17   18   19
end;
```

Implementation

```
   function Find_Aux is new Regular_Lists.Find(Test);
begin
  S.Current := Find_Aux(Item, S.Current);
end Find;
```

10.5.20 FIND_IF

Specification

```
generic
     with function Test(X : Element) return Boolean;
procedure Find_If(S : in out Del);
```

Description   If S contains an element E such that Test(E) is true, at
the current element or beyond, then the current element is set to the
leftmost such element; otherwise the current element pointer falls off the
end of S.

Time   order nm

Space   0

> **where** $n = $ length(S)and m is the average time for Test

Mutative?   No

Shares?   No

See also   Find, Find_If_Not, Some, Search

Examples

```
declare
  Temp : Del;
  procedure Find_If_Greater_Than_7 is
     new Find_If(Test => Greater_Than_7);
begin
  Iota(15, Temp);
  Find_If_Greater_Than_7(Temp);
  Show_List(Temp);
--   8  9  10  11  12  13  14
end;
```

Implementation

```
   function Find_Aux is new Regular_Lists.Find_If(Test);
begin
  S.Current := Find_Aux(S.Current);
end Find_If;
```

10.5.21   FIND_IF_NOT

Specification

```
generic
     with function Test(X : Element) return Boolean;
procedure Find_If_Not(S : in out Del);
```

Description   If S contains an element E such that Test(E) is false, at the current element or beyond, then the current element is set to the leftmost such element; otherwise the current element pointer falls off the end of S.

Time   order nm

Space   0

   where $n = \text{length(S)}$ and m is the average time for Test

Mutative?   No

Shares?   No

See also   Find, Find_If, Some, Search

Examples

```
declare
  Temp : Del;
  procedure Find_If_Not_Greater_Than_7 is
      new Find_If_Not(Test => Greater_Than_7);
begin
  Iota(15, Temp);
  Invert(Temp);
  Initialize(Temp);
  Find_If_Not_Greater_Than_7(Temp);
  Show_List(Temp);
--  7 6 5 4 3 2 1 0
end;
```

Implementation

```
   function Find_Aux is new Regular_Lists.Find_If_Not(Test);
begin
  S.Current := Find_Aux(S.Current);
end Find_If_Not;
```

10.5.22   FIRST

Specification

```
function First(S : Del)
       return Element;
pragma inline(First);
```

Description   Returns the first (left-most) element of S.

Time   constant

Space   0

Mutative?   No

Shares?   No

Details   Attempts to apply the generic formal First even if S has no elements.

See also

Implementation

```
begin
  return First(S.First);
end First;
```

10.5.23 FOR_EACH

Specification

```
generic
      with procedure The_Procedure(X : Element);
procedure For_Each(S : Del);
```

Description   Applies The_Procedure to each element of S starting with the current element and going to the end.

Time   order np

Space   0

> **where** $n = $ length(S)and p is the average time for The_Procedure

Mutative?   No

Shares?   No

See also   For_Each_2, Map

Implementation

```
   procedure For_Each_Aux is
         new Regular_Lists.For_Each(The_Procedure);
begin
  For_Each_Aux(S.Current);
end For_Each;
```

10.5.24   FOR_EACH_2

Specification

```
generic
      with procedure The_Procedure(X, Y : Element);
procedure For_Each_2(S1, S2 : Del);
```

Description   Applies The_Procedure to pairs of elements of S1 and S2 in the same position, starting with the current elements and going to the end.

Time   order np

Space   0

where p is the average time for The_Procedure, $n = \min(n_1, n_2)$, $n_1 = \text{length}(S1)$, $n_2 = \text{length}(S2)$

Mutative?   No

Shares?   No

Details   Stops when the end of either S1 or S2 is reached.

See also   For_Each, Map, Map_2

Implementation

```
procedure For_Each_Aux is
      new Regular_Lists.For_Each_2(The_Procedure);
begin
  For_Each_Aux(S1.Current, S2.Current);
end For_Each_2;
```

10.5.25 FREE

Specification

```
procedure Free(S : in out Del);
pragma inline(Free);
```

Description   Causes the storage cells occupied by S to be made available for reuse.

Time   order n

Space   0 (makes space available)

> **where** $n = \text{length}(S)$

Mutative?   Yes

Shares?   No

Details   The header record of S is retained, but is made empty.

See also

Implementation

```
begin
  Regular_Lists.Free_Sequence(S.First);
  Make_Empty(S);
end Free;
```

10.5.26 INITIALIZE

Specification

```
procedure Initialize(S : in out Del);
pragma inline(Initialize);
```

Description   The current element of S is reset to the first element.

Time   constant

Space   0

Mutative?   No

Shares?   No

See also   Make_Empty

Implementation

```
begin
  S.Current := S.First;
end Initialize;
```

10.5.27 INVERT

Specification

```
procedure Invert(S : in out Del);
```

Description   Modifies S to contain the same elements as its input value, but in reverse order.

Time   order n

Space   0

   where $n = \text{length}(S)$

Mutative?   Yes

Shares?   No

Details   The element referred to by the current element is the same as before the inversion, but its position is changed: if initially it was i, the new current element position is $n - 1 - i$.

See also

Examples

```
declare
  Temp : Del;
begin
  Iota(6, Temp);
  Invert(Temp);
  Initialize(Temp);
  Show_List(Temp);
-- 5 4 3 2 1 0
end;
declare
  Temp : Del;
begin
  Invert(Temp);
  Show_List(Temp);

end;
```

Implementation

```
  Temp : Sequence := Regular_Lists.Invert(S.First);
begin
  S.Last := S.First;
  S.First := Temp;
end Invert;
```

10.5.28   IS_EMPTY

Specification

```
function Is_Empty(S : Del)
       return Boolean;
pragma inline(Is_Empty);
```

Description   Returns true if S has no elements, false otherwise.

Time   constant

Space   0

Mutative?   No

Shares?   No

See also   Is_End

Implementation

```
begin
  return Regular_Lists.Is_End(S.First);
end Is_Empty;
```

10.5.29   Is_End

Specification

```
function Is_End(S : Del)
        return Boolean;
pragma inline(Is_End);
```

Description   Returns true if the current element of S has fallen off the end, false otherwise.

Time   constant

Space   0

Mutative?   No

Shares?   No

See also   Is_Empty

Implementation

```
begin
  return Regular_Lists.Is_End(S.Current);
end Is_End;
```

10.5.30 LAST

Specification

```
function Last(S : Del)
        return Element;
pragma inline(Last);
```

Description   Returns the last element of S.

Time   constant

Space   0

Mutative?   No

Shares?   No

Details   Attempts to apply the generic formal First even if S is empty.

See also   First, Current

Implementation

```
begin
  return First(S.Last);
end Last;
```

10.5.31   LENGTH

Specification

```
function Length(S : Del)
      return Integer;
```

Description   Returns the number of elements in S from the current element to the end, as a non-negative integer.

Time   constant

Space   0

Mutative?   No

Shares?   No

Details   The current element is included in the count.

See also

Implementation

```
begin
  return Regular_Lists.Length(S.Current);
end Length;
```

10.5.32 MAP

Specification

```
generic
      with function F(E : Element) return Element;
procedure Map(S : Del);
```

Description   Modifies S to consist of the results of applying F to each element of S, from the current element to the end.

Time   order nf

Space   order n

where $n = \text{length(S)}$ and f is the average time for F

Mutative?   Yes

Shares?   No

See also   For_Each

Examples

```
declare
  Temp : Del;
  procedure Map_Square is new Map(F => Square);
begin
  Iota(5, Temp);
  Map_Square(Temp);
  Show_List(Temp);
-- 0  1  4  9  16
end;
```

Implementation

```
  Dummy : Sequence;
  function Map_Aux is new Regular_Lists.Map(F);
begin
  Dummy := Map_Aux(S.Current);
end Map;
```

10.5.33 MAP_2

Specification

```
generic
      with function F(X, Y : Element) return Element;
procedure Map_2(S1, S2 : Del);
```

Description   Modifies S1 to be a sequence of the results of applying F to corresponding elements of S1 and S2, starting with the current elements and going to the end.

Time   order nf

Space   order n

where $n_1 = \text{length}(S1)$, $n_2 = \text{length}(S2)$, $n = \min(n_1, n_2)$, and f is the average time for F

Mutative?   Yes

Shares?   No

Details   Let $X_0, X_1, \ldots, X_{n_1-1}$ be the elements of S1 and $Y_0, Y_1, \ldots, Y_{n_2-1}$ be those of S2. The new value of S1 computed by Map_2 consists of $F(X_0,Y_0)$, $F(X_1,Y_1)$, ..., $F(X_{n-1},Y_{n-1})$, where $n = \min(n_1, n_2)$.

See also   For_Each

Examples

```
declare
  Temp_1, Temp_2 : Del;
  procedure Map_2_Times is new Map_2(F => "*");
begin
  Iota(5, Temp_1);
  Iota(5, Temp_2);
  Invert(Temp_2);
  Initialize(Temp_2);
  Map_2_Times(Temp_1, Temp_2);
  Show_List(Temp_1);
--  0  3  4  3  0
end;
```

Implementation

```
  Dummy : Sequence;
  function Map_2_Aux is new Regular_Lists.Map_2(F);
begin
  Dummy := Map_2_Aux(S1.Current, S2.Current);
end Map_2;
```

10.5.34   MERGE

Specification

```
generic
      with function Test(X, Y : Element) return Boolean;
procedure Merge(S1, S2 : in out Del);
```

Description   Modifies S1 to be a sequence containing the same elements as S1 and S2, interleaved. If S1 and S2 are in order as determined by Test, then the result will be also. Both S1 and S2 are mutated.

Time   order $(n_1 + n_2)m$

Space   order $n_1 + n_2$

   where $n_1 = \text{length}(S1)$, $n_2 = \text{length}(S2)$, and m is the average time for Test

Mutative?   Yes

Shares?   No

Details   By "interleaved" is meant that if X precedes Y in S1 then X will precede Y in the new S1 and similarly for X and Y in S2 (even if S1 or S2 is not in order). The property of stability also holds. See Section 6.1.7 for discussion of the restrictions on Test and definition of "in order as determined by Test."

See also   Sort, Concatenate

Examples

```
declare
  Temp_1, Temp_2 : Del;
  procedure Shuffle_Merge is
      new Merge(Test => Shuffle_Test);
begin
  Iota(5, Temp_1);
  Iota(5, Temp_2);
  Invert(Temp_2);
  Initialize(Temp_2);
  Shuffle_Merge(Temp_1, Temp_2);
  Show_List(Temp_1);
--  0  4  1  3  2  2  3  1  4  0
end;
```

Implementation

```
   function Merge_Aux is new Regular_Lists.Merge(Test);
begin
  Put_List(S1, Merge_Aux(S1.First, S2.First));
  Make_Empty(S2);
end Merge;
```

10.5.35   MISMATCH

Specification

```
generic
     with function Test(X, Y : Element) return Boolean;
procedure Mismatch(S1, S2 : in out Del);
```

Description   S1 and S2 are scanned in parallel, starting from their current elements, until the first position is found at which they disagree, using Test as the test for element equality. S1 and S2 have their current elements set to the elements at which the first disagreement occurs.

Time   order $\min(n_1, n_2)m$

Space   0

where $n_1 = \text{length(S1)}$ and $n_2 = \text{length(S2)}$ and m is the average time for Test

Mutative?   No

Shares?   No

Details   S1 and S2 both have their current pointers set off the end if S1 and S2 agree entirely.

See also   Equal

Implementation

```
    Temp_1, Temp_2 : Sequence;
    procedure Mismatch_Aux is
        new Regular_Lists.Mismatch(Test);
  begin
    Mismatch_Aux(S1.Current, S2.Current, Temp_1, Temp_2);
    S1.Current := Temp_1;
    S2.Current := Temp_2;
  end Mismatch;
```

10.5.36 NOT_ANY

Specification

```
generic
     with function Test(X : Element) return Boolean;
function Not_Any(S : Del)
        return Boolean;
```

Description   Returns true if Test is false of every element of S, from its current element on, false otherwise. Elements numbered i, $i + 1$, $i + 2$, ... are tried in order, where the i-th element is current.

Time   order nm

Space   0

where $n = \text{length}(S)$ and m is the average time for Test

Mutative?   No

Shares?   No

Details   Returns true if the current element is off the end.

See also   Every, Some, Not_Every

Examples

```
declare
  Temp : Del;
  function Not_Any_Odd is new Not_Any(Test => Odd);
begin
 Iota(10, Temp);
  Show_Boolean(Not_Any_Odd(Temp));
-- False
end;
declare
  Temp : Del;
  function Not_Any_Odd is new Not_Any(Test => Odd);
  procedure Delete_If_Odd is new Delete_If(Test => Odd);
begin
  Iota(10, Temp);
  Delete_If_Odd(Temp);
  Show_Boolean(Not_Any_Odd(Temp));
-- True
end;
```

Implementation

```
   function Not_Any_Aux is new Regular_Lists.Not_Any(Test);
begin
   return Not_Any_Aux(S.Current);
end Not_Any;
```

10.5.37   NOT_EVERY

Specification

```
generic
     with function Test(X : Element) return Boolean;
function Not_Every(S : Del)
        return Boolean;
```

Description   Returns true if Test is false of some element of S, from its current element on, false otherwise. Elements numbered i, i + 1, i + 2, ... are tried in order, where the i-th element is current.

Time   order nm

Space   0

   where $n = $ length(S)and m is the average time for Test

Mutative?   No

Shares?   No

Details   Returns false if the current element of S is off the end.

See also   Every, Some

Examples

```
declare
  Temp : Del;
  function Not_Every_Odd is new Not_Every(Test => Odd);
begin
  Iota(10, Temp);
  Show_Boolean(Not_Every_Odd(Temp));
--   True
end;
declare
  Temp : Del;
  function Not_Every_Odd is new Not_Every(Test => Odd);
  procedure Delete_If_Not_Odd is
       new Delete_If_Not(Test => Odd);
begin
  Iota(10, Temp);
  Delete_If_Not_Odd(Temp);
  Show_Boolean(Not_Every_Odd(Temp));
--   False
end;
```

Implementation

```
   function Not_Every_Aux is
       new Regular_Lists.Not_Every(Test);
begin
   return Not_Every_Aux(S.Current);
end Not_Every;
```

10.5.38   REDUCE

Specification

```
generic
      Identity : Element;
  with function F(X, Y : Element) return Element;
function Reduce(S : Del)
      return Element;
```

Description   Combines all the elements of S using F, from the current element on; for example, using "+" for F and 0 for Identity one can add up a sequence of Integers.

Time   order nm

Space   0

> where $n = \text{length}(S)$ and m is the average time for Test

Mutative?   No

Shares?   No

See also   For_Each, Map

Examples

```
declare
  Temp : Del;
  function Reduce_Times is
      new Reduce(Identity => 1, F => "*");
begin
  Iota(5, Temp);
  Advance(Temp);
  Show_Integer(Reduce_Times(Temp));
--  24
end;
declare
  Temp : Del;
  function Reduce_Plus is
      new Reduce(Identity => 0, F => "+");
begin
  Iota(100, Temp);
  Show_Integer(Reduce_Plus(Temp));
--  4950
end;
```

Implementation

```
function Reduce_Aux is
    new Regular_Lists.Reduce(Identity, F);
begin
  return Reduce_Aux(S.Current);
end Reduce;
```

10.5.39   SEARCH

Specification

```
generic
      with function Test(X, Y : Element) return Boolean;
   procedure Search(S1 : Del; S2 : in out Del);
```

Description   Searches S2, starting with the current element, for the left-most occurrence of a subsequence that element-wise matches S1, using Test as the test for element-wise equality, and moves the current element pointer of S2 to this subsequence. If no matching subsequence is found, the current element pointer of S2 is set off the end.

Time   order nm

Space   0

where $n = $ length(S)and m is the average time for Test

Mutative?   No

Shares?   No

See also   Position, Find, Some, Search

Examples

```
declare
   Temp_1, Temp_2 : Del;
   procedure Search_Equal is new Search(Test => "=");
begin
   Add_Last(7, Temp_1);
   Add_Last(8, Temp_1);
   Add_Last(9, Temp_1);
   Iota(12, Temp_2);
   Search_Equal(Temp_1, Temp_2);
   Show_List(Temp_2);
-- 7 8 9 10 11
end;
```

Implementation

```
   function Search_Aux is new Regular_Lists.Search(Test);
begin
   S2.Current := Search_Aux(S1.Current, S2.Current);
end Search;
```

10.5.40 SET_CURRENT

Specification

```
procedure Set_Current(S : Del; X : Element);
pragma inline(Set_Current);
```

Description   S is modified by replacing its current element by X.

Time   constant

Space   0

Mutative?   Yes

Shares?   No

Details   Attempts to apply the generic formal Set_First even if the current element pointer is off the end of S.

See also   Current, Set_First

Implementation

```
begin
  Set_First(S.Current, X);
end Set_Current;
```

10.5.41   SET_FIRST

Specification

```
procedure Set_First(S : Del; X : Element);
pragma inline(Set_First);
```

Description   S is modified by replacing its first element by X.

Time   constant

Space   0

Mutative?   Yes

Shares?   No

Details   Attempts to apply the generic formal Set_First even if Is_End is true of the first element pointer of S (which can only be true of S has no elements).

See also   Current, Set_First

Implementation

```
begin
  Set_First(S.First, X);
end Set_First;
```

10.5.42 SET_LAST

Specification

```
procedure Set_Last(S : Del; X : Element);
pragma inline(Set_Last);
```

Description S is modified by replacing its last element by X.

Time constant

Space 0

Mutative? Yes

Shares? No

Details Attempts to apply the generic formal Set_First even if Is_End is true of the last element pointer of S (which can only be true of S has no elements).

See also Current, Set_First

Implementation

```
begin
  Set_First(S.Last, X);
end Set_Last;
```

10.5.43 SOME

Specification

```
generic
      with function Test(X : Element) return Boolean;
function Some(S : Del)
        return Boolean;
```

Description   Returns true if Test is true of some element of S, from the current element on, false otherwise. Elements numbered i, i + 1, i + 2, ... are tried in order, where the i-th element is current.

Time   order nm

Space   0

where $n = $ length(S)and m is the average time for Test

Mutative?   No

Shares?   No

Details   Returns false if the current element of S is off the end.

See also   Not_Every, Every, Not_Any

Examples

```
declare
  Temp : Del;
  function Some_Odd is new Some(Test => Odd);
begin
  Iota(10, Temp);
  Show_Boolean(Some_Odd(Temp));
True
end;
declare
  Temp : Del;
  function Some_Odd is new Some(Test => Odd);
  procedure Delete_If_Odd is new Delete_If(Test => Odd);
begin
  Iota(10, Temp);
  Delete_If_Odd(Temp);
  Show_Boolean(Some_Odd(Temp));
False
end;
```

Implementation

```
  function Some_Aux is new Regular_Lists.Some(Test);
begin
  return Some_Aux(S.Current);
end Some;
```

10.5.44   SORT

Specification

```
generic
      with function Test(X, Y : Element) return Boolean;
   procedure Sort(S : in out Del);
```

Description   Modifies S to be a sequence containing the same elements as S, but in order as determined by Test.

Time   order $(n \log n)m$

Space   0

   where $n = \text{length(S)}$ and m is the average time for Test

Mutative?   Yes

Shares?   No

Details   This is a stable sort. See Section 6.1.7 for discussion of the restrictions on Test and definition of "in order as determined by Test."

See also   Merge

Examples

```
declare
   Temp_1, Temp_2 : Del;
   procedure Sort_Ascending is new Sort(Test => "<");
   procedure Shuffle_Merge is
       new Merge(Test => Shuffle_Test);
begin
   Iota(5, Temp_1);
   Iota(5, Temp_2);
   Invert(Temp_2);
   Initialize(Temp_2);
   Shuffle_Merge(Temp_1, Temp_2);
   Sort_Ascending(Temp_1);
   Show_List(Temp_1);
-- 0  0  1  1  2  2  3  3  4  4
end;
```

Implementation

```
   function Sort_Aux is new Regular_Lists.Sort(Test);
begin
   Put_List(S, Sort_Aux(S.First));
   end Sort;
```

10.5.45 SPLIT

Specification

```
procedure Split(S1, S2 : in out Del);
pragma inline(Split);
```

Description   S1 is split into two parts: all elements up to and including its current element (this becomes the new value of S1) and all elements following the current element of S1 (this becomes the new value of S2).

Time   constant

Space   0

Mutative?   Yes

Shares?   No

Details   Procedure Free is applied to the input value of S2. The current element of the new S1 is its last element and of the new S2 is its first element.

See also   Concatenate

Examples

```
declare
  Temp_1, Temp_2 : Del;
begin
  Iota(4, Temp_1);
  Advance(Temp_1);
  Split(Temp_1, Temp_2);
  Initialize(Temp_1);
  Show_List(Temp_2);
--  2  3
  Show_List(Temp_1);
--  0  1
end;
```

Implementation

```
   Next_One : Sequence;
begin
  Free(S2);
  if not Is_End(S1) then
    Next_One := Next(S1.Current);
    if not Regular_Lists.Is_End(Next_One) then
      Set_Next(S1.Current, Nil);
      S2.First := Next_One;
      S2.Current := Next_One;
      S2.Last := S1.Last;
      S1.Last := S1.Current;
    end if;
  end if;
end Split;
```

10.5.46 SUBSTITUTE

Specification

```
generic
      with function Test(X, Y : Element) return Boolean;
   procedure Substitute(New_Item, Old_Item: Element; S: Del);
```

Description   Modifies S so that, from the current element on, the elements E such that Test(Old_Item,E) is true are replaced by New_Item.

Time   order nm

Space   0

where $n = $ length(S)and m is the average time for Test

Mutative?   Yes

Shares?   No

See also   Substitute_If, Substitute_If_Not

Examples

```
declare
  Temp : Del;
  procedure Substitute_When_Divides is
      new Substitute(Test => Divides);
begin
  Iota(15, Temp);
  Substitute_When_Divides(-1, 3, Temp);
  Show_List(Temp);
-- -1  1  2 -1  4  5 -1  7  8 -1  10  11 -1  13  14
end;
```

Implementation

```
  Dummy : Sequence;
  function Substitute_Aux is
      new Regular_Lists.Substitute(Test);
begin
  Dummy := Substitute_Aux(New_Item, Old_Item, S.Current);
end Substitute;
```

10.5.47   SUBSTITUTE_IF

Specification

```
generic
     with function Test(X : Element) return Boolean;
procedure Substitute_If(New_Item : Element; S : Del);
```

Description   Modifies S so that, from the current pointer on, the elements E such that Test(E) is true are replaced by New_Item.

Time   order nm

Space   0

where $n = $ length(S)and m is the average time for Test

Mutative?   Yes

Shares?   No

See also   Substitute_If_Not, Substitute

Examples

```
declare
  Temp : Del;
  procedure Substitute_If_Odd is
      new Substitute_If(Test => Odd);
begin
  Iota(15, Temp);
  Substitute_If_Odd(-1, Temp);
  Show_List(Temp);
--   0 -1  2 -1  4 -1  6 -1  8 -1  10 -1  12 -1  14
end;
```

Implementation

```
  Dummy : Sequence;
  function Substitute_If_Aux is
      new Regular_Lists.Substitute_If(Test);
begin
  Dummy := Substitute_If_Aux(New_Item, S.Current);
end Substitute_If;
```

10.5.48   SUBSTITUTE_IF_NOT

Specification

```
generic
     with function Test(X : Element) return Boolean;
procedure Substitute_If_Not(New_Item : Element; S : Del);
```

Description   Modifies S so that, from the current pointer on, the elements E such that Test(E) is false are replaced by New_Item.

Time   order nm

Space   0

> where n = length(S)and m is the average time for Test

Mutative?   Yes

Shares?   No

See also   Substitute_If_Not, Substitute

Examples

```
declare
  Temp : Del;
  procedure Substitute_If_Not_Odd is
     new Substitute_If_Not(Test => Odd);
begin
  Iota(15, Temp);
  Substitute_If_Not_Odd(-1, Temp);
  Show_List(Temp);
-- -1  1 -1  3 -1  5 -1  7 -1  9 -1  11 -1  13 -1
end;
```

Implementation

```
  Dummy : Sequence;
  function Substitute_If_Not_Aux is
     new Regular_Lists.Substitute_If_Not(Test);
begin
  Dummy := Substitute_If_Not_Aux(New_Item, S.Current);
end Substitute_If_Not;
```

11

Stacks Package

This package provides one of the simplest of linear data structures, in which insertions and deletions of data are restricted to one end. Its name suggests the most appropriate model for understanding its behavior: a stack of papers on a desk, which can only be changed by placing a sheet of paper on top or by removing one from the top, and the one on top is the only one whose information can be examined. Another frequently used term for a stack discipline is "Last-In First-Out" (LIFO).

11.1 Package specification

The package specification is as follows:

```
generic
  type Element  is private;
  type Sequence is private;
  with procedure Create(S: out Sequence);
  with function Full(S: Sequence) return Boolean;
  with function Empty(S: Sequence) return Boolean;
  with function First(S: Sequence) return Element;
  with function Next(S: Sequence) return Sequence;
  with function Construct(E: Element; S: Sequence)
      return Sequence;
  with procedure Free_Construct(S : Sequence);
package Stacks is
  type Stack is limited private;
  Stack_Underflow, Stack_Overflow : exception;

 {The subprogram specifications}

  private
  type Stack is new Sequence;

end Stacks;
```

11.2 Package body

The package body is as follows:

```
package body Stacks is

 {The subprogram bodies}

 end Stacks;
```

11.3   Definitions for the examples

The following definitions are referenced in the examples included in the
subprogram descriptions. (This is the skeleton of a test suite in which the
examples are included.)

```
with Stacks_1; -- a PIP;
package Integer_Stacks is new Stacks_1(Integer);

with Integer_Stacks, Text_Io, Examples_Help;
procedure Test_Stacks is
  use Integer_Stacks.Inner, Text_Io, Examples_Help;

  procedure Show_Stack(S : in out Stack) is
    procedure Show_Stack_Aux is
        new For_Each(Print_Integer);
  begin
    Put("--:"); Show_Stack_Aux(S); New_Line;
  end Show_Stack;

begin


  {Examples from the subprograms}


  Show("End Of Tests");
end;
```

11.4   Subprograms

11.4.1   CREATE

Specification

```
procedure Create(S : out Stack);
pragma inline(Create);
```

Description   Makes S be an empty stack.

Time   constant

Space   0

Mutative?   Yes

Shares?   No

See also   Push, Pop

Examples

```
-- See Push
```

Implementation

```
begin
  Create(Sequence(S));
end Create;
```

11.4.2 FOR_EACH

Specification

```
generic
with procedure The_Procedure(E : Element);
procedure For_Each(S: in out Stack);
pragma inline(For_Each);
```

Description Successively removes each element E of S, from the top down, and applies The_Procedure to E.

Time order np

Space 0

   where n is the number of elements in the stack, and p is the average time for The_Procedure

Mutative? Yes

Shares? No

Details Does nothing if S is empty. If an unhandled exception is raised while executing The_Procedure on an element, those elements that were below it are left in S.

See also Pop, Top

Examples

```
-- See Push
```

Implementation

```
  An_Element: Element;
begin
  while not Is_Empty(S) loop
    Pop(An_Element, S);
    The_Procedure(An_Element);
  end loop;
end For_Each;
```

11.4.3   IS_EMPTY

Specification

```
function Is_Empty(S : Stack)
      return Boolean;
pragma inline(Is_Empty);
```

Description   Returns true if S has no elements in it, false otherwise.

Time   constant

Space   0

Mutative?   No

Shares?   No

See also   Push, Pop

Examples

```
-- See Push
```

Implementation

```
begin
  return Empty(Sequence(S));
end Is_Empty;
```

11.4.4   POP

Specification

```
procedure Pop(The_Element : out Element; S : in out Stack);
pragma inline(Pop);
```

Description   Causes the top element of S to be removed and returned as the value of The_Element.

Time   constant

Space   0

Mutative?   Yes

Shares?   No

Details   Raises an exception, Stack_Underflow, if S is empty.

See also   Push, Top

Examples

```
-- See Push
```

Implementation

```
  Old : Sequence := Sequence(S);
begin
  if Empty(Sequence(S)) then raise Stack_Underflow;
  end if;
  The_Element := Top(S);
  S := Stack(Next(Sequence(S)));
  Free_Construct(Old);
end Pop;
```

11.4.5 PUSH

Specification

```
procedure Push(The_Element : in Element; S : in out Stack);
pragma inline(Push);
```

Description   Places The_Element on top of S.

Time   constant

Space   constant

Mutative?   Yes

Shares?   No

Details   Raises an exception, Stack_Overflow, if S is already full.

See also   Pop, Top

Examples

```
declare
   S : Stack; E : Integer;
 begin
   Create(S);
   Push(2, S); Push(3, S); Push(5, S); Push(7, S);
   Show_Integer(Top(S));
-- 7
   Pop(E, S);
   Show_Integer(E);
-- 7
   Show_Integer(Top(S));
-- 5
   Show_Boolean(Is_Empty(S));
-- False
   Show_Stack(S);
-- 5 3 2
   Show_Boolean(Is_Empty(S));
-- True
 end;
```

Implementation

```
begin
  if Full(Sequence(S)) then raise Stack_Overflow;
  end if;
  S := Stack(Construct(The_Element, Sequence(S)));
end Push;
```

11.4.6 TOP

Specification

```
function Top(S : Stack)
       return Element;
pragma inline(Top);
```

Description   Returns the top element of S, without removing it.

Time   constant

Space   0

Mutative?   No

Shares?   No

Details   Raises an exception, Stack_Underflow, if S is empty.

See also   Pop, Push

Examples

```
-- See Push
```

Implementation

```
begin
  if Is_Empty(S) then raise Stack_Underflow;
  end if;
  return First(Sequence(S));
end Top;
```

12

Output Restricted Deques Package

A *deque* is a linear data structure consisting of finite sequences in which insertions and deletions are permitted only at the ends. Thus stacks and queues can be viewed as special cases of deques that have further restrictions on accesses: a stack prohibits both insertions and deletions at one end, while a queue can only have insertions at one end and only deletions at the other. One of the least restricted cases of a deque is that in which both insertions and deletions are permitted at one end (called the front), but at the other end (the rear) only insertions are allowed; hence it is called *output-restricted*. This package provides such a data structure, as a representational abstraction.

The generic parameters of the package are types and subprograms that allow the package to be easily plugged together with Double_Ended_Lists, but the parameters also could be satisfied with a vector representation of sequences.

12.1   Package specification

The package specification is as follows:

```
generic
  type Element  is private;
  type Sequence is limited private;
  with procedure Create(S: in out Sequence);
  with function Full(S: Sequence) return Boolean;
  with function Empty(S: Sequence) return Boolean;
  with function First(S: Sequence) return Element;
  with function Last(S: Sequence) return Element;
  with procedure Add_First(E: Element;
      S: in out Sequence);
  with procedure Add_Last(E: Element;
      S: in out Sequence);
  with procedure Drop_First(S: in out Sequence);
package Output_Restricted_Deques is
  type Deque is limited private;
  Deque_Underflow, Deque_Overflow: exception;
```

```
{The subprogram specifications}

  private
  type Deque is new Sequence;
end Output_Restricted_Deques;
```

12.2   Package body

The package body is as follows:

```
package body Output_Restricted_Deques is

  {The subprogram bodies}

end Output_Restricted_Deques;
```

12.3   Definitions for the examples

The following definitions are referenced in the examples included in the
subprogram descriptions. (This is the skeleton of a test suite in which the
examples are included.)

```
with Output_Restricted_Deques_1;  -- a PIP
package Integer_Output_Restricted_Deques is new
    Output_Restricted_Deques_1(Integer);
with Integer_Output_Restricted_Deques, Text_Io,
    Examples_Help;
procedure Test_Deques is
  use Integer_Output_Restricted_Deques.Inner,
    Text_Io, Examples_Help;

  procedure Show_Deque(D : in out Deque) is
  -- note that this makes D empty;
    procedure Show_Deque_Aux is
        new For_Each(Print_Integer);
  begin
    Put("--:"); Show_Deque_Aux(D); New_Line;
  end Show_Deque;
begin
  {Examples from the subprograms}

  Show("End Of Tests");
end;
```

12.4   Subprograms

12.4.1   CREATE

Specification

```
procedure Create(D : in out Deque);
pragma inline(Create);
```

Description   Makes D be an empty deque.

Time   constant

Space   0

Mutative?   Yes

Shares?   No

See also

Examples

```
-- See Push_Front
```

Implementation

```
begin
  Create(Sequence(D));
end Create;
```

12.4.2   FOR_EACH

Specification

```
generic
  with procedure The_Procedure(E : Element);
procedure For_Each(D: in out Deque);
pragma inline(For_Each);
```

Description   Successively removes each element E of D, from the front to the rear, and applies The_Procedure to E.

Time   order np

Space   0

   where n is the number of elements in D, and p is the average time for The_Procedure

Mutative?   Yes

Shares?   No

Details   Does nothing if D is empty. If an unhandled exception is raised while executing The_Procedure on an element, those elements that were after it (from front to rear) are left in the deque.

See also

Examples

```
-- See Push_Front
```

Implementation

```
  An_Element: Element;
begin
  while not Is_Empty(D) loop
    Pop_Front(An_Element, D);
    The_Procedure(An_Element);
  end loop;
end For_Each;
```

12.4.3 FRONT

Specification

```
function Front(D : Deque)
      return Element;
pragma inline(Front);
```

Description   Returns the front element of D, without removing it.

Time   constant

Space   0

Mutative?   No

Shares?   No

Details   Raises an exception, Deque_Underflow, if D is empty.

See also   Pop_Front, Push_Front

Examples

```
-- See Push_Front, Push_Rear
```

Implementation

```
begin
  if Is_Empty(D) then raise Deque_Underflow;
  end if;
  return First(Sequence(D));
end Front;
```

12.4.4   Is_Empty

Specification

```
function Is_Empty(D : Deque)
        return Boolean;
pragma inline(Is_Empty);
```

Description   Returns true if D has no elements in it, false otherwise.

Time   constant

Space   0

Mutative?   No

Shares?   No

See also   Push_Front, Push_Rear, Pop_Front

Examples

```
-- See Push_Front
```

Implementation

```
begin
  return Empty(Sequence(D));
end Is_Empty;
```

12.4.5   POP_FRONT

Specification

```
procedure Pop_Front(The_Element: out Element;
    D: in out Deque);
pragma inline(Pop_Front);
```

Description   Causes the front element of D to be removed and returned as the value of The_Element.

Time   constant

Space   0

Mutative?   Yes

Shares?   No

Details   Raises an exception, Deque_Underflow, if D is empty.

See also   Push_Front, Front

Examples

```
-- See Push_Front, Push_Rear
```

Implementation

```
begin
  if Empty(Sequence(D)) then raise Deque_Underflow;
  else
    The_Element := Front(D);
    Drop_First(Sequence(D));
  end if;
end Pop_Front;
```

12.4.6   PUSH_FRONT

Specification

```
procedure Push_Front(The_Element: in Element;
    D: in out Deque);
pragma inline(Push_Front);
```

Description   Places The_Element on the front of D.

Time   constant

Space   constant

Mutative?   Yes

Shares?   No

Details   Raises an exception, Deque_Overflow, if D is already full.

See also   Pop_Front, Front

Examples

```
declare
  D : Deque; E : Integer;
begin
  Create(D);
  Push_Front(2, D); Push_Front(3, D); Push_Front(5, D);
      Push_Front(7, D);
  Show_Integer(Front(D));
-- 7
  Pop_Front(E, D);
  Show_Integer(E);
-- 7
  Show_Integer(Front(D));
-- 5
  Show_Boolean(Is_Empty(D));
-- False
  Show_Deque(D);
-- 5 3 2
  Show_Boolean(Is_Empty(D));
-- True
end;
```

Implementation

```
begin
  if Full(Sequence(D)) then raise Deque_Overflow;
  end if;
  Add_First(The_Element, Sequence(D));
end Push_Front;
```

12.4.7   PUSH_REAR

Specification

```
procedure Push_Rear(The_Element: in Element;
    D: in out Deque);
pragma inline(Push_Rear);
```

Description   Places The_Element on the rear of D.

Time   constant

Space   constant

Mutative?   Yes

Shares?   No

Details   Raises an exception, Deque_Overflow, if D is already full.

See also   Rear

Examples

```
declare
  D : Deque; E : Integer;
begin
  Push_Rear(2, D); Push_Rear(3, D); Push_Rear(5, D); Push_Rear(7, D);
  Show_Integer(Rear(D));
--  7
  Pop_Front(E, D);
  Show_Integer(E);
--  2
  Show_Integer(Front(D));
--  3
  Show_Boolean(Is_Empty(D));
-- False
  Show_Deque(D);
--  3  5  7
  Show_Boolean(Is_Empty(D));
--  True
end;
```

Implementation

```
begin
  if Full(Sequence(D)) then raise Deque_Overflow;
  end if;
  Add_Last(The_Element, Sequence(D));
end Push_Rear;
```

12.4.8 REAR

Specification

```
function Rear(D : Deque)
      return Element;
pragma inline(Rear);
```

Description   Returns the rear element of D, without removing it.

Time   constant

Space   0

Mutative?   No

Shares?   No

Details   Raises an exception, Deque_Underflow, if D is empty.

See also   Push_Rear

Examples

```
-- See Push_Rear
```

Implementation

```
begin
  if Is_Empty(D) then raise Deque_Underflow;
  end if;
  return Last(Sequence(D));
end Rear;
```

13

Using the Packages

13.1 Partially instantiated packages

The purpose of each of these packages, called "PIPs," is to plug together
a low-level data abstraction package with a structural or representational
abstraction package, while leaving the **Element** type (and perhaps other parameters) generic. In Part 1 we showed PIPs obtained from combining each
of three low-level representations of singly-linked-lists with the **Singly_-
Linked_Lists** structural abstraction. For each of the representational abstractions in Chapters 10, 11, and 12, there are three three PIPs included
in the library for plugging the representational abstraction together with a
particular low-level representation.

13.1.1 PIPs for Double Ended Lists

From file delpip1.ada--

```
with System_Allocated_Singly_Linked, Double_Ended_Lists;
generic
   type Element is private;
package Double_Ended_Lists_1 is

   package Low_Level is
      new System_Allocated_Singly_Linked(Element);
   use Low_Level;

   package Inner is
     new Double_Ended_Lists(Element, Sequence, Nil, First,
       Next, Construct, Set_First, Set_Next, Free);

end Double_Ended_Lists_1;--
```

From file delpip2.ada--

```
with User_Allocated_Singly_Linked, Double_Ended_Lists;
generic
   Heap_Size : in Natural;
   type Element is private;
package Double_Ended_Lists_2 is
```

```
  package Low_Level
    is new User_Allocated_Singly_Linked(Heap_Size, Element);
  use Low_Level;

  package Inner is
    new Double_Ended_Lists(Element, Sequence, Nil, First,
        Next, Construct, Set_First, Set_Next, Free);

end Double_Ended_Lists_2;--
```

From file delpip3.ada--

```
  with Auto_Reallocating_Singly_Linked, Double_Ended_Lists;
generic
  Initial_Number_Of_Blocks : in Positive;
  Block_Size               : in Positive;
  Coefficient              : in Float;
  type Element is private;
package Double_Ended_Lists_3 is

  package Low_Level is new
    Auto_Reallocating_Singly_Linked(Initial_Number_Of_Blocks,
                          Block_Size, Coefficient, Element);
  use Low_Level;

  package Inner is
    new Double_Ended_Lists(Element, Sequence, Nil, First,
        Next, Construct, Set_First, Set_Next, Free);

end Double_Ended_Lists_3;--
```

13.1.2   PIPs for Stacks

In this case the low-level representation provided by System_Allocated_-
Singly_Linked does not provide exactly the operations needed by Stacks,
but appropriate definitions of the missing operations (Create, Full, and
Empty) are easily specified in the package specification and programmed
in the package body.

From file stackpl.ada--

```
      with System_Allocated_Singly_Linked, Stacks;
generic
  type Element is private;
package Stacks_1 is

  package Low_Level is
```

```
      new System_Allocated_Singly_Linked(Element);
   use Low_Level;

   procedure Create(S : out Sequence);
   pragma inline(Create);
   function Full(S : Sequence) return Boolean;
   pragma inline(Full);
   function Empty(S : Sequence) return Boolean;
   pragma inline(Empty);

   package Inner is
      new Stacks(Element, Sequence, Create, Full, Empty,
         First, Next, Construct, Free);

end Stacks_1;


package body Stacks_1 is

   use Low_Level;
   procedure Create(S : out Sequence) is
   begin
      S := Nil;
   end Create;

   function Full(S : Sequence) return Boolean is
   begin
      return False;   -- Stacks are unbounded when
                      -- represented as singly-linked-lists;
   end Full;

   function Empty(S : Sequence) return Boolean is
   begin
      return S = Nil;
   end Empty;

end Stacks_1;--
```

The other two PIPs, Stacks_2 and Stacks_3 for for plugging Stacks
together with User_Allocated_Singly_Linked and Auto_Reallocating_-
Singly_Linked, respectively, are similar to Stacks_1.

13.1.3 PIPs for Output Restricted Deques

Another twist to the construction of PIPs is introduced here. The operations needed by Output_Restricted_Deques are conveniently supplied by Double_Ended_Lists, so we use an instance of a PIP for Double_Ended_Lists as the low-level representation. Since, as in the PIP for Stacks, not all of the operations needed are supplied directly, two are specified and programmed in this PIP's specification and body.

From file outdeqp1.ada--

```
        with Double_Ended_Lists_1, Output_Restricted_Deques;
generic
  type Element is private;
package Output_Restricted_Deques_1 is

  package Low_Level is new Double_Ended_Lists_1(Element);
  use Low_Level.Inner;

  function Full(D : Del) return Boolean;
  pragma inline(Full);
  procedure Drop_First(D : in out Del);
  pragma inline(Drop_First);

  package Inner is new
    Output_Restricted_Deques(Element, Del, Free,
    Full, Is_Empty, First, Last, Add_First,
    Add_Last, Drop_First);

end Output_Restricted_Deques_1;

package body Output_Restricted_Deques_1 is
  use Low_Level.Inner;

  function Full(D : Del) return Boolean is
  begin
    return False;   -- double-ended-lists are unbounded when
                    -- represented as singly-linked-lists;
  end Full;

  procedure Drop_First(D : in out Del) is
  begin
    Initialize(D);
    Drop_Head(D);
  end Drop_First;

end Output_Restricted_Deques_1;--
```

Similar PIPs, which are called **Output_Restricted_Deques_2** and **Output_-Restricted_Deques_3**, are provided for plugging **Output_Restricted_Deques** together with **User_Allocated_Singly_Linked** and **Auto_Reallocating_-Singly_Linked**, respectively.

13.2   Test suites and output

Test suites are produced from the test suite package skeletons given in the chapters on the packages and the examples given with each subprogram.

The output that is produced is indicated in the comments in those examples.

Appendix A

Examples Help Package

The following package defines a few procedures and functions that aid in the construction of examples and test cases for the various packages.

From file examhelp.ada--

```ada
package Examples_Help is

-- I/O procedures

  procedure Print_Integer(I : in Integer);
  procedure Show(The_String : String);
  procedure Show_Boolean(B : Boolean);
  procedure Show_Integer(I : Integer);

-- Some other little functions needed to construct examples

  function Divides(A, B : Integer) return Boolean;
  function Even(A : Integer) return Boolean;
  function Odd(A : Integer) return Boolean;
  function Greater_Than_7(A : Integer) return Boolean;
  function Square(A : Integer) return Integer;

end Examples_Help;

with Text_Io; use Text_Io;
package body Examples_Help is

-- I/O procedures

  procedure Print_Integer(I : in Integer) is
  begin
    Put(Integer'Image(I));
    Put(" ");
  end Print_Integer;

  procedure Show(The_String : String) is
  begin
    Put(The_String); New_Line;
  end Show;
```

```
  procedure Show_Boolean(B : Boolean) is
  begin
    if B then
      Show("--: True");
    else
      Show("--: False");
    end if;
  end Show_Boolean;

  procedure Show_Integer(I : Integer) is
  begin
    Put("--:"); Print_Integer(I); New_Line;
  end Show_Integer;

-- Some other little functions needed to construct examples

  function Divides(A, B : Integer) return Boolean is
  begin
    return B mod A = 0;
  end Divides;

  function Even(A : Integer) return Boolean is
  begin
    return Divides(2, A);
  end Even;

  function Odd(A : Integer) return Boolean is
  begin
    return not Divides(2, A);
  end Odd;

  function Greater_Than_7(A : Integer) return Boolean is
  begin
    return A > 7;
  end Greater_Than_7;

  function Square(A : Integer) return Integer is
  begin
    return A * A;
  end Square;

end Examples_Help;--
```

Appendix B

Combining Stacks with a Vector Representation

The `Stacks` and `Output_Restricted_Deques` packages can be combined with low-level representations other than linked lists, since the generic parameters of these packages do not need all of the characteristics of linked-lists (in particular, no `Set_Next` operation is needed). In order to give a concrete illustration of this point, we show a simple representation of vectors that supplies the operations needed for instantiation of `Stacks`.

B.1   Simple_Indexed_Vectors package specification

From file sivects.ada--

```
generic

  Max_Size : in Natural;
  type Element is private;

package Simple_Indexed_Vectors is

  type Sequence is private;
  procedure Create(S: in out Sequence);
  function Full(S: Sequence) return Boolean;
  function Empty(S: Sequence) return Boolean;
  function First(S: Sequence) return Element;
  function Next(S: Sequence) return Sequence;
  function Construct(E: Element; S: Sequence)
      return Sequence;
  procedure Free_Construct(S: Sequence);

private

  type Node;
  type Sequence is access Node;

end Simple_Indexed_Vectors;--
```

B.2   Simple_Indexed_Vectors package body

From file sivectb.ada--

```
package body Simple_Indexed_Vectors is

type Storage is
    array(Integer range 1 .. Max_Size) of Element;

type Node is record
   Vector_Field : Storage;
   Index_Field  : Integer range 0 .. Max_Size := 0;
  end record;

procedure Create(S : in out Sequence) is
begin
  S := new Node;
end Create;

function Full(S : Sequence) return Boolean is
begin
  return (S.Index_Field = Max_Size);
end Full;

function Empty(S : Sequence) return Boolean is
begin
  return (S.Index_Field = 0);
end Empty;

function First(S : Sequence) return Element is
begin
  return S.Vector_Field(S.Index_Field);
end First;

function Next(S : Sequence) return Sequence is
begin
  S.Index_Field := S.Index_Field - 1;
  return S;
end Next;

function Construct(E: Element;
    S: Sequence) return Sequence is
begin
  S.Index_Field := S.Index_Field + 1;
  S.Vector_Field(S.Index_Field) := E;
```

```
    return S;
  end Construct;

  procedure Free_Construct(S : Sequence) is
  begin
    null;
  end Free_Construct;

  end Simple_Indexed_Vectors;--
```

B.3   A PIP combining Vectors and Stacks

From file stackp4.ada--

```
  with Simple_Indexed_Vectors, Stacks;
  generic
    Max_Size : in Natural;
    type Element is private;
  package Stacks_4 is

    package Low_Level is
        new Simple_Indexed_Vectors(Max_Size, Element);
    use Low_Level;

    package Inner is
        new Stacks(Element, Sequence, Create, Full,
      Empty, First, Next, Construct, Free_Construct);

  end Stacks_4;--
```

DISKETTE ORDERING INSTRUCTIONS

The source files for the Ada packages described in this book are available in machine–readable form, on 5 1/4 inch diskette.

Please note that compilation with a PC based Ada compiler is probably *not* possible, based on difficulties that have been encountered with several such compilers. Using the diskette and a communications program such as Kermit, one may transfer the files to a VAX or other computer on which they may be compiled. A sample command file is included for compiling the packages with the Digital Equipment Corporation VAX Ada compiler. One other compiler known to be capable of compiling the packages correctly is the Sun Ada Compiler (also known as the Telesoft Ada Compiler) running on Sun Microsystems Workstations.

The diskette is 5 1/4 inch double-sided/double density. It operates on DOS 2.0/3.0/4.0 on IBM PC, XT, AT, and IBM compatible machines.

The address for ordering the diskette is:

> Ada Generic Libraries
> c/o Springer Verlag New York
> Computer Science Editorial
> 175 Fifth Avenue
> New York, New York 10010

For orders to be sent to a U.S. or Canadian address, send a check or money order for $20.00 in U.S. funds or the equivalent in Canadian funds, payable to Ada Generic Libraries. New York residents please add appropriate sales tax. For addresses outside the U.S. or Candada, send $25.00 in U.S. funds. These prices are subject to change.

Postage and shipping charges are included in the above amounts. Only diskettes with manufacturing defects may be returned for replacement (no cash refunds).

Please note that this volume contains the complete source code for the packages described; the purpose of the diskette is merely to make it available in machine–readable form. The authors and publisher make no warranties, expressed or implied, that the software contained in this volume or on the diskettes is free of error, or is consistent with any particular standard of mechantability or fitness for a particular purpose.

Technical questions or corrections should be directed to the above address.